TABLE OF CONTENTS
'History of the Deep State'
Jeremy Stone

CHAPTER 1: THIRTEEN COLONIES   4

SECTION 1.1   Cornwallis & Washington
SECTION 1.2   Deep State Global Banking system
SECTION 1.3   Kabbalistic Deep State Invasion

CHAPTER 2: JFK: PATRIOT & REBEL   26

SECTION 2.1   Secret societies threatened
SECTION 2.2   JFK Deep and the Deep State
SECTION 2.3   JFK And the Federal Reserve

CHAPTER 3: THE ILLUMINATI   66

SECTION 3.1   The Old Order
SECTION 3.2   American Revolution & The Deep State

CHAPTER 4: ANCIENT SYMBOLISM   94

SECTION 4.1   Origin of the Great Seal

SECTION 4.2   MSM Mind Control

CHAPTER 5: MILITARY INDUSTRIAL COMPLEX   116

SECTION 5.1   Eisenhower's dire Warning

SECTION 5.2   Operation Paperclip

SECTION 5.3   Nazi Infiltration of the U.S.

CHAPTER 6: THE BAVARIAN BLOODLINE   136

SECTION 6.1   The romans, illuminati, & the Nazis
SECTION 6.2   The Old Order vs the New Order

CHAPTER 7: THE C.F.R. 154
SECTION 7.1 C.F.R.'S PLAN TO ELIMINATE NATIONALISM

SECTION 7.2 GLOBALIZED COMMUNISM

CHAPTER 8: THE NEW WORLD ORDER 173

SECTION 8.1 HITLER'S ENHANCEMENT OF THE OLD ORDER

SECTION 8.2 THE NEW WORLD ORDERS PLANS FOR 2020

CHAPTER ONE
THIRTEEN COLONIES

What if I told you that nearly everything you have learned in academia, most of what you have experienced in your life, as it pertains to politics and social sciences, and many of the political conclusions you have formed using critical thinking, is a lie? Even what you partially understand to be the truth about politics is most likely just an amalgamation of disinformation and half-truths, disseminated by The Deep State.

Obama was a Communist as were the Bushes, they are both related, and through the bloodline of Kings; elected to utilize a rigged system of psychological tactics, black magic, and mind control propaganda to

5 | HISTORY OF THE DEEP STATE

influence your vote. You may be tempted to hurl this book across the room now, but after you finish this thorough explanation of The Deep State, and its many components of confusion, dissemination, infiltration, compartmentalization, and ultimately its goal of destroying the fabric of our country from within, you will experience a disturbing but necessary paradigm shift; and your anger will gradually shift from the disturbing truths revealed in this book to the outrage at being lied to for so many years by the monstrous and well-oiled machine known as The Deep State.

The term Deep State refers to an internal and foreign Government that functions independently and in direct opposition to our sovereign Nation State. This kind of shadow government is both internal and foreign because although its members currently function inside nearly every U.S. Government agency, they are foreign, as they operate as embedded moles from previous administrations and have been inserted from hostile foreign governments in an attempt to undermine our Republic, with their ultimate goal being to replace our Nationalist State with a Globalist-Communist State.)

The Communist/foreign State and Deep State are interchangeable terms, in that this foreign state was devised by the Council of Foreign Relations, or CFR, and have been financed by the Rockefeller Foundation, which will be explained in detail in subsequent chapters.

The Deep State is also a global enterprise with many complex components extending into world affairs, with operations outside of The United States; but to gain a complete understanding of the origins of the Deep State, we must begin with the foundation of the United States and then work backwards, since the American model is the apex of all previous models.

CORNWALLIS & WASHINGTON

"A general dissolution of principles and manners will more surely overthrow the liberties of America than the whole force of the

HISTORY OF THE DEEP STATE

common enemy. While the people are virtuous they cannot be subdued; but when once they lose their virtue then will be ready to surrender their liberties to the first external or [internal invader]."

- *Samuel Adams, letter to James Warren, February 12, 1779*

The Revolutionary war was the most important battle for freedom from despotism and oppression the world will ever know; only World War II rivals it. Freedom is not free, and the American spirit could not be better exemplified than through the perseverance, opposition, revolt and our ultimate defeat of the strongest military in the world at that time.

The early rebel soldiers did not even utilize a traditional military when confronting the British army at Lexington Green, but were effectively militiamen or 'street fighters,' and the penalty for treason against the British Army was severing the hands and feet, disembowelment, then death by hanging.

Ironically, the British army had similar struggles with the American minutemen against the British Empire, who were by this time a corrupt, heavily indebted, despotic and quasi-socialist State; ruling with an iron fist. The British Monarchy was hungry, not so much for land or power, as they were to collect money from the colonists who, as they saw it, were merely debt slaves.

To pay back loans from Dutch, British, and East India Company bankers, where The British Empire had accrued a national debt that nearly doubled from 75 million pounds in 1754 to 133 million in 1763, collecting their money by force became their last and final resort at making good with their financiers. Taxing American colonists on goods and merchandise at a high rate and applying unfair and outrageous tariffs on exports was unreasonable and understandably unwarranted, as American patriots saw it, we were being governed in tyranny from a Foreign Government

HISTORY OF THE DEEP STATE

thousands of miles across the Atlantic Ocean.

"WHAT WE MEANT IN GOING FOR THOSE REDCOATS WAS THIS: WE ALWAYS HAD BEEN FREE, AND WE MEANT TO BE FREE ALWAYS! THEY DIDN'T MEAN THAT WE SHOULD."

- REBEL CAPTAIN, LEVI PRESTON

BRITISH GLOBALIST BANKING SYSTEM NEVER RESOLVED

"The real truth of the matter is, as you and I know, that a financial element in the larger centers has owned the Government ever since the days of Andrew Jackson — and I am not wholly excepting the Administration of W. W. The country is going through a repetition of Jackson's fight with the Bank of the United States — only on a far bigger and broader basis."

- Franklin D. Roosevelt

"Banks have done more injury to the religion, morality, tranquility, prosperity, and even wealth of the nation than they can have done or ever will do good."

- John Adams

"If the American people ever allow private banks to control the issue of their currency, first by inflation, then by deflation, the banks and corporations that will grow up around them will deprive the people of all property until their children wake up homeless on the continent their Fathers conquered...I believe that banking institutions are more dangerous to our liberties than standing armies... The issuing power should be taken from the banks and restored to the people, to whom it properly belongs."
  - Jefferson 1802

The Industrial Revolution in Britain was booming at the turn of the 18th century and was ripe for the exploitation of the emerging

11 | HISTORY OF THE DEEP STATE

factory and mill markets. Although Holland was dominant in the 17th century with regard to keeping their investments at home and within their own banks during the beginning of the industrial revolution, over time British markets and investors were able to usurp the revenue from Holland, which it acquired during the Industrial revolution by housing the only dominate banking system in Europe, which Holland used, making Britain a pollical superpower.

The same banking families that originated in Britain who dominated Hollands finances, and spoils of the industrial revolution during the 17th and 18th century, by 1776 maintained its dominance and influence in America.(Those same families still dominate all twelve federal reserve bank branches today.)According to CPA Thomas D. Schauf, only ten banks and banking families control the 12 Federal Reserve Bank branches:

Rothschild Bank of Berlin, Lazard Brothers of Paris, Warburg Bank of Hamburg, Warburg Bank of Amsterdam, Lehman Brothers of New York, N.M. Rothschild of

London, Lazard Brothers of Paris, Kuhn Loeb Bank of New York, Kuhn Loeb Bank of New York, Israel Moses Seif Bank of Italy, Goldman Sachs of New York and JP Morgan's Chase Bank of New York.

The 13 known Illuminati families are either also one of these ten banking families or indirectly influencing them, and they are as follows:

THE ASTOR BLOODLINE

THE BUNDY BLOODLINE

THE COLLINS BLOODLINE

THE DUPONT BLOODLINE

THE FREEMAN BLOODLINE

THE KENNEDY BLOODLINE

The Li Bloodline

The Onassis Bloodline

The Reynolds Bloodline

The Rockefeller Bloodline

The Rothschild Bloodline

The Russell Bloodline

The Van Duyn Bloodline

As you can see the Illuminati have been running Governments through financial manipulation and blackmail, including our own, from the foundation of our nation's history. The banking system is just one of many components which The Deep State utilizes to obtain their short-term goals and long-term New World Order objective.

Without getting into too much detail, it is important to briefly outline that the British conceded their territory and rights to America but left behind their corrupt and foreign Banking system. The British knew there would be no escaping their shadowy and manipulative Deep State financial control and manipulation they would exert over us, even before the British/American truce and the signing of the Treaty of Paris. Since 1776 we have been trying, to no avail, through a sequence of theoretical trial and error systems, to find a workaround this Globalized Banking epidemic. Here are the failed Global banking systems used since 1791:

THE FIRST BANK OF THE UNITED STATES
1791-1811

The First Bank of The United States was a private banking institution which was 70 percent foreign-owned, moreover, its stock was traded and dominated by both domestic and foreign investors.

THE SECOND BANK OF THE UNITED STATES 1816-1836

1829 – Jackson becomes President, vetoing the bill for the early re-charter of The Second Bank of the U.S.

Jan 30, 1835 – Attempted Assassination of Andrew Jackson

1833-1837 – Artificial Economic Boom Created by Illuminati Banking Families

1837-1843 – Panic of 1837, Economic Collapse

1862-1863 – Lincoln Issues Greenbacks, effectively removing Foreign Banking influence In America

April 15, 1865 – Lincoln Assassinated by Illuminati

1881- Advocate of U.S Currency Backed by Gold and Silver, President James Garfield, Assassinated.

1907- The Banking Panic of 1907

1908 – Nelson Aldrich (Rockefeller Relative & JP Morgan Partner) becomes Head of New National Monetary Commission

1910 – Illuminati family Bankers Meet in Secret at Jekyll Island Drafting the Federal Reserve Act

The Illuminati bankers in attendance:

Nelson Aldrich, A.P. Andrew (Assistant Secretary of the Treasury), Frank Vanderlip (President of National City Bank of New York), Paul Warburg (Kuhn, Loeb, & Co.), Henry Davidson (Senior Partner of JP Morgan

Co.), Charles D. Norton (President of JP Morgan's First National Bank of New York) and Benjamin Strong (JP Morgan Partner).

THIRD CENTRAL BANK: Federal Reserve System 1913- Present Day

1921-1929 Federal Reserve Banking overwhelms the U.S. Economy with Money and loans

October 24, 1929 – Stock Market Crash

1930 -1941 – The Great Depression

June 4, 1963 – Kennedy Signs an Executive Order Authorizing the US Treasury to Issue Silver Certificates

Nov. 22, 1963 – JFK Assassination

December 1963 – Lyndon Johnson undoes Kennedy's Executive Order Authorizing Issuing of Silver Certificates

The globalized influence of our Federal Reserve Banks is the foundation of the Deep State. If it's ever compromised or threated, someone will have to pay for all the corrupt money that has been invested into it. On the surface, it may appear that 'The Gold Standard' works, so it is therefore thwarted by nefarious financiers. It is not the gold substitute that upsets global financiers and bankers, but the fact that Gold would substitute their Foreign influence. Foreign financiers own the very banks that have manipulated our Federal Reserve, allowing these 13 Illuminati banking families to control markets, manipulate events, cause inflation, and devalue our currency. The founding fathers foresaw this as a serious National Security threat from hostile foreign actors (these hostile foreign actors later went so far as to finance the insertion of Communists into our Government agencies and Communism into our schools and culture (Explained further in later chapters). Our Banking system has been problematic from the beginning. The elimination of unfettered meddling in our economy has been an epidemic for two hundred and forty years. Trying to find a perfect solution seems nearly impossible at this point, even JP Morgan worked with the Rothchild's to bring in foreign gold to be used for our gold standard!

Unfortunately, this flaw in our economy caused hostile infiltration of the worst kind, corruption at every conceivable level and agency of our Government, and as society becomes increasingly unethical, pushing the boundaries of sickness and depravity, the schemes to undermine our Country will only get worse. President Trump has rightfully addressed many of these issues, but as for the future - only time will tell how many more Presidents after him can weather this Deep State storm.

"Some of the biggest men in the United States are afraid of something. They know there is a power somewhere, so organized, so subtle, so watchful, so interlocked, so complete, so pervasive that they had better not speak above their breath when they speak in condemnation of it."
- President Woodrow Wilson

A Kabbalists system had flaws which were warned against by the Founding Fathers

Our Founding Fathers were Kabbalists. The number 13 is significant in the Kabbalah and the Masonic Bible, the evidence supporting this is apparent when examining the many clues that they left behind. The significance of numerology can be found throughout the inception of our country.

There were 13 Colonies, not by chance, but by design. The Declaration of Independence was intentionally planned to be pronounced on July 4th, 1776, which is sixty-six days after the highest Pagan Holy day (Witch's Day

[The Pagan Summer Solstice]) April 30th, 1776. Independence Day is also precisely thirteen days after [The Christian Summer Solstice] June 21st, 1776.

What is the significance of tying both the Pagan and Christian Summer solstice together on Independence Day? The answer lies at the core of what both Free Masons and Kabbalists believe, and the author will leave it to the reader to decide whether it is good or evil.

Both 13 and 66 are highly significant Kabbalistic numbers and play a role in the 'Sacred Geometry' introduced to and passed down through Pagan societies since the Babylonians.

This type of knowledge has been kept secret because, although it can be perceived as Satanic, for Kabbalists, it holds an extraordinary power which they found useful in the formations of successful Governments throughout recorded history.

The connection and significance to the July 4th, 1776 as it relates to these seemingly strange patterns of numerology are not accidental or happenstance, instead they were calculated for an esoteric but authentic application of traditional knowledge passed down through ancient Babylon, ancient Egypt, into the Roman Empire, The British Empire, and inevitably into The United States. All successful Empires following this same pattern which the founding fathers were invariable aware of and could not escape.

"For God doth know that in the day ye eat thereof, then your eyes shall be opened, and ye shall be as gods, knowing good and evil."
- *Genesis 3:5*

Since Good opposes evil, when placing them inside Government and politics, two things occur. One, it creates an atmosphere similar to the dichotomy of man's nature, which possesses the knowledge of both good and evil. How this knowledge is applied and the degrees to which it is used could mean the difference between the acquisition of extraordinary power with the built-in possibility of destroying itself.

I have coined this phenomenon with the terminology used in cyber security known as a 'logic bomb.' Effectively a logic bomb is simply a virus which is preset to destroy a machine once the required conditions are met. Within a Government with two warring and opposing sides, the conditions

necessary to execute a 'logic bomb' are an overwhelming and uncontrollable evil prevailing in every aspect of society.

This type of internal threat has been discussed and warned about by our founding fathers, specifically as it relates to a two-party system in Government:

"There is nothing which I dread so much as a division of the republic into two great parties, each arranged under its leader, and

concerting measures in opposition to each other. This, in my humble apprehension, is to be dreaded as the greatest political evil under our Constitution."

- *JOHN ADAMS, October 2, 1789*

George Washington takes the idea further, as a prediction:

"However [political parties] may now and then answer popular ends, they are likely in the course of time and things, to become potent engines, by which cunning, ambitious, and unprincipled men will be enabled to subvert the power of the people and to usurp for themselves the reins of government, destroying afterwards the very engines which have lifted them to unjust dominion."

- *GEORGE WASHINGTON, September 19, 1796*

CHAPTER TWO
J.F.K. PATRIOT & REBEL

"FOR WE ARE OPPOSED AROUND THE WORLD BY A MONOLITHIC AND RUTHLESS CONSPIRACY THAT RELIES PRIMARILY ON COVERT MEANS FOR EXPANDING ITS SPHERE OF INFLUENCE--ON INFILTRATION INSTEAD OF INVASION, ON SUBVERSION INSTEAD OF ELECTIONS, ON INTIMIDATION INSTEAD OF FREE CHOICE, ON GUERRILLAS BY NIGHT INSTEAD OF ARMIES BY DAY. IT IS A SYSTEM WHICH HAS CONSCRIPTED VAST HUMAN AND MATERIAL RESOURCES INTO THE BUILDING OF A TIGHTLY KNIT, HIGHLY EFFICIENT MACHINE THAT COMBINES MILITARY, DIPLOMATIC, INTELLIGENCE, ECONOMIC, SCIENTIFIC AND POLITICAL OPERATIONS. ITS PREPARATIONS ARE CONCEALED, NOT PUBLISHED. ITS MISTAKES ARE BURIED, NOT HEADLINED. ITS DISSENTERS ARE SILENCED, NOT PRAISED. NO EXPENDITURE IS QUESTIONED, NO RUMOR IS PRINTED, NO SECRET IS REVEALED."

- PRESIDENT JOHN F KENNEDY

When John F. Kennedy was sworn in on January 20th, 1961 what he had inherited from previous administrations was not just daunting, but some would say an impossible array of crises that any mortal President could ever hope to fix. Although many of these problems began in fact, years earlier, as staged crises, they had nevertheless become very real. From the Vietnam war to Cuba, the Cold War, fighting Communism around the globe, safeguarding the Federal Reserve banking system from outside and foreign influence, to fighting Secret Societies inside our own Government Agencies; there would be no way out, if not for John F Kennedys great Patriotism and Rebellion from a bloodline and tradition which, he himself descended. Since previous Presidents allowed these problems to foment, they kicked the can down the road in fear, perhaps hoping someone greater would come, brave enough to face The Deep State head on and finally clean up the mess. That man was John F. Kennedy.

SECRET SOCIETIES THREATENED

27 | HISTORY OF THE DEEP STATE

Few people know or want to know, that John F. Kennedy was in fact directly related to one of the thirteen Illuminati families. Kennedy's Father was a third-degree Illuminati member, at the top of the Illuminati's Pilgrim Society, (still the most powerful, exclusive, and influential of any of the Secret Societies around the world to date) comprised of elite members such as the Rockefellers, JP Morgan, the Vanderbilt's, Skull and Bones, The Knights Templar, and head investors of The Federal Reserve.

Joseph Patrick Kennedy Sr. paved the way for John F Kennedy's Presidency, being a Democrat with a lot of power, political influence and heavily financed. Joe made his fortune by acquiring and merging major Hollywood movie studios and working with organized crime families, bootlegging moonshine throughout the United States during and after the days of Prohibition. Mob boss, Frank Costello famously said, "I helped Joe Kennedy get rich."

"If Kathleen and her husband were living, I'd be the father of the Duchess of Devonshire and the father-in-law of the head of all the Masons in the World".
– Joseph P. Kennedy

President Franklin D. Roosevelt, 33rd degree Mason, high-ranking Illuminati member, and the Grand Master of the Order of DeMolay; was frequently advised by Joe Kennedy and is often referred to as the unofficial Ambassador between the United States and Britain before World War II. After private meetings with Nazi Germany, Joe was suspected by both U.S. and British governments to be a Nazi sympathizer for making anti-Semitic remarks. This coupled with his relentless push to keep U.S. military participation outside of Nazi Germany made him suspect, and ultimately led to his prominent role as an advisor being diminished on both sides. Despite this, Joe Kennedy Sr. maintained his status among the Royal Monarchy in Great Britain and his dominance among the Secret Societies of the world. To say that Joseph Kennedy was influential among the Illuminati and the ruling class elite, would be an understatement; he, in fact, remains the highest-ranking Illuminati member in recent times.

FIGHTING COMMUNISM AROUND THE WORLD

"I realize that this Nation often tends to identify turning-points in world affairs with the major addresses which preceded them. But it was not the Monroe Doctrine that kept all Europe away from this hemisphere—it was the strength of the British fleet and the width of the Atlantic Ocean. It was not General Marshall's speech at Harvard which kept Communism out of Western Europe—it was the strength and stability made possible by our military and economic assistance... We in this country, in this generation, are—by destiny rather than choice – the watchmen on the walls of world freedom."

- John F Kennedy (The Speech JFK never gave)

CUBA AND THE USSR

Fidel Castro's was on the CIA's and intelligence agencies radar long before the Vietnam War when President Batista still held power in Cuba, The Deep State fomented, allowed and planned to put Castro into power, which they accomplished by 1959. This was allowed for the purpose of solving the very same problem they had created. Fomenting crises to provide a military solution for the crisis later is still a regular practice of The Deep State.

Being a Communist, Castro would naturally align himself with the Soviet Union. The Soviets helped Cuba with economic and military aid. The truth about The Bay of Pigs and The Cuban Missile Crisis is a sick and perverted one. Predicting Castro's rise to power a decade prior did not take a super intelligent CIA agent or think tank to see it coming, it was easily foreseeable that Castro, being a Communist, would naturally align

HISTORY OF THE DEEP STATE

himself with the prominent Communist Country and our enemy at the time, the U.S.S.R. This would then would cause an alliance of two Communist states, one, Cuba, being right off of our shores!

The Deep State allowing and even facilitating a Cuban/U.S.S.R. alliance is unthinkable for many people, that is until you understand why they do it. The Military Industrial Complex, or MIC, (which I will discuss at length in a later chapter) essentially is a Military machine that foreign Governments, investors, and prominent Illuminati members use as a tool to profit from war. Why were our intelligence agencies involved? Because they were working for those very same institutions, as Communists. Now before you may think this implausible, I will also outline this in later chapters but, in short, proof of this can be found in the Smoot report and that the Rockefellers were infiltrating our Country for decades with Communism and Communists.

History tells us that the CIA was planning to send U.S. military trained Cuban exiles through an inlet into Cuba, known as the Bay of Pigs. This mission was planned before the facilitation of Castro's rise to power, during the Eisenhower administration. Simply put, The Cuban Missile Crisis could have been averted by eliminating Castro's regime by dispatching Fidel Castro early on. Although today our Government is restricted from conducting such operations without military involvement, during that time, however, the United States Government could legally assassinate whoever has deemed a threat to our national security. If this were appropriately utilized, we would not have had a Communist Cuban Missile Crisis to deal with later.

Eisenhower was informed by the CIA and the intelligence community a decade prior, about this foreseeable crisis, and how it planned to handle it, with a United States/Cuban War, after it became a full-blown crisis. This may be one of the reasons why Eisenhower implied about a Military Industrial Complex being a grave threat to National Security as

33 | HISTORY OF THE DEEP STATE

he left office, during his Farewell Address to the Nation in 1961.

When Kennedy took office in 1961, he as subsequently notified about this decade-long Military plan to oust Castro using military force. Kennedy did not like the idea, and instead proposed a clandestine operation of an invasion of Cuba via the Bay of Pigs. Without going into great detail here, The CIA agreed to Kennedy's solution; however, it would secretly not allow their MIC investments to be thwarted. Hence, he was double-crossed by The Deep State, who alerted the U.S.S.R. and Cuba of Kennedy's intentions to invade The Bay of Pigs secretly; causing the very Cuban exiles Kennedy had trained by the CIA, to be captured. Approximately 1,500 Cuban exiled fighters were imprisoned during the Bay of Pigs invasion, giving President Kennedy a black eye making him a very unpopular president.

The Kennedy Administration took responsibility for the failure of the Bay of Pigs failure, of course, although he was not accountable for being double-crossed by The Deep State. Shortly after that, the Soviet Union had stockpiled Cuba, and the Communist Castro Regime with nuclear ballistic missiles, which the Soviets claimed was an effort to defend against a U.S. preemptive strike.

The pinnacle of the Cold War was during a 13-day period during October 1962, known as 'The Cuban Missile Crisis.' Kennedy and Khrushchev were embroiled in a tense 13-day nuclear showdown just off the coast of Cuba. Kennedy had, by that time deployed a U-2 spy plane to conduct a covert reconnaissance operation, verifying the presence of a fully operational nuclear facility in Cuba. The Soviets transported Nuclear arms to Cuba in retaliation for the U.S. Nuclear facility based in Turkey. Both opposing countries short-range missiles were within striking distance of the each other. A full-scale nuclear war was never more eminent than during these 13 days, as Kennedy established a Naval blockade halting the Soviet transport of more Nuclear armaments to Communist Cuba.

Because a working communication system between The United States and the Soviet Union had diminished during the Cold War prior to this mounting crisis it was necessary for both Governments to communicate using letters and other slow-paced forms of communications, causing malaise and public distress about the possibility of any misstep could quickly escalate into an all-out Nuclear War within a matter of minutes. However, on October 28, Kennedy was given the message by Khrushchev, offering to remove their missiles in Cuba, with the condition that the U.S. must also surrender their missiles from Turkey with the assurance that we would not invade Cuba. A full-scale nuclear war had been averted, narrowly and by the skin of its teeth.

KENNEDY WAS SECRETLY PULLING TROOPS OUT OF VIETNAM

We must expand upon The Deep State's version of history as it relates to President Kennedy's supposed failures in fighting Communism, by rewriting history, as it actually happened. If one were to read most any Historical account of Kennedy's involvement in fighting Communism, we are effectively learning from the Deep States smears and blackmail of John F Kennedy. It is appalling how much disinformation remains throughout academia, textbooks, and the internet.

The misrepresentation of Kennedys fight against Communism is due in part by the Deep States double crossing JFK at the Bay of Pigs, mischaracterizing him as a failure. The truth is, The Deep State has been a long-time proponent of Communism as a way to destroy Governments from within. Smearing Kennedys efforts to destroy Communism would take any focus off of the collective

37 | HISTORY OF THE DEEP STATE

Communist influence inside our intelligence agencies, and permanently damaging his chances of being reelected had he lived through 1964.

Kennedy's battle with Communism was both an external and internal one. The external fight was not only against the Communist U.S.S.R and Cuba, at the Bay of Pigs (which would have been a success had he not been compromised by the Deep State) and finding a workable solution for The Cuban Missile Crisis involving the Soviets; Kennedy secretly signed an executive order, pulling troops out of Vietnam before the Vietnam War, when the United States involvement in Vietnam was beginning to take shape as a Police action in 1962. The Executive order signed by Kennedy removed around 1,500 troops from Vietnam.

However, JFK's executive order was immediately reversed by his successor President Johnson. Johnson not only re-stationed our Military police action presence in Vietnam but as you know, started 'The

Unwinnable Vietnam War.' The term 'Unwinnable War' was not a theory. It was understood by military Generals and intel that war to be fought in the jungle with an enemy using Guerilla tactical warfare was sending soldiers into slaughter. While this was not directly fighting Communism for Kennedy, it was a fight for America Patriotism. The only reason to engage in a ten-year war which in the and would prove unwinnable would be to continue to amass an incredible Military budget year after year, mostly profiting companies like Lockheed Martin and various other private wartime producing companies, who were heavily invested in profiting from it. These Illuminati banking families were profiting from what President Eisenhower foretold and warned against when detailing the perils of the Military Industrial Complex in 1961.

Incredibly, all of this is not discussed regarding JFK's legacy, nor is it sited whatsoever in United States history; But, there's more. Fighting internal Communism is one of JFK's most clandestine and

HISTORY OF THE DEEP STATE

unknown operations of all. John F Kennedy was very good friends with Joseph McCarthy, as was his father Joseph Kennedy Sr. Some of the photographs of the both of them seen together have been either scrubbed from the Internet or buried. It is my personal belief and can also be substantiated by various other authors on JFK that The President was conducting yet another covert operation to purge Communists from further infiltrating the activities of Deep State Government, Hollywood, and Main Stream Media Propaganda during Kennedys Presidency.

The degree to which they were successful in stopping the spread of internal communism from our culture and Government agencies is not quantifiable. However, there are some notable quotes by McCarthy and Robert J. Lamphere that give us some insight into the magnitude of the corruption and infiltration of Deep State Communists embedded into various Government agencies before and during President John F Kennedys tenure in office:

"While I cannot take the time to name all the men in the State Department who have been named as members of the Communist Party and members of a spy ring, I have here in my hand a list of 205—a list of names that were known to the secretary of State and who, nevertheless, are still working and shaping policy of the State Department"
- Joseph McCarthy

Robert Lamphere, Contact for the United States Army's Signal Intelligence Service's VENONA program:

"There were a lot of spies in the Government, but not all in the State Department."
- Robert J. Lamphere

WHO KILLED JFK?

The subject of exactly who killed JFK and how, is one that could quickly fill a small encyclopedia, but I will attempt to summarize it as much as possible. More importantly,

HISTORY OF THE DEEP STATE

why was John F Kennedy assassinated? Who had the motivation to do it? I will start with who killed Kennedy, then work backward; from the bottom of the Illuminati pyramid working our way to the top.

It is the author's opinion that there were most likely several assassins, one of the men involved at the bottom ~~was~~ of the pyramid was Joseph Milteer. Mitleer was a wealthy member of the Illuminati with ties to very powerful Deep State agents. Without going into too much detail, On November 9th, 1963, William Somerset, a Government informant, questioned Joseph Milteer personally and recorded their conversation:

Somerset: "I think Kennedy is coming here on the 18th, or something like that to make some kind of speech . . ."

Milteer: "You can bet your bottom dollar he is going to have a lot to say about the Cubans. There are so many of them here."

Somerset: "Yeah. Well, he will have a thousand bodyguards, don't worry about that."

Milteer: "The more bodyguards he has the easier it is to get him."

Somerset: "Well, how in the hell do you figure would be the best way to get him?"

Milteer: "From an office building with a high-powered rifle. How many people does he have going around who look just like him? Do you now about that?"

Somerset: "No, I never heard he had anybody."

Milteer: "He has about fifteen. Whenever he goes anyplace, he knows he is a marked man."

Somerset: "You think he knows he is a marked man?"

Milteer:" Sure, he does."

Somerset: "They are really going to try to kill him?"

Milteer: "Oh yeah, it is in the working. Brown himself, Brown is just as likely to get him as anybody in the world. He hasn't said so, but he tried to get Martin Luther King."

Somerset: "Boy, if that Kennedy gets shot, we have to know where we are at. Because you know that will be a real shake if they do that."

Milteer: "They wouldn't leave any stone unturned there, no way. They will pick somebody up within hours afterwards, if anything like that would happen. Just to throw the public off."

It is clear from this exchange between Somerset, and the informant Milteer is giving us definite clues as to how Kennedy would be assassinated. He also claims that 'The more bodyguards (Kennedy) has, the easier it is to get him", suggesting that other assassins were embroiled in the plot to kill Kennedy, namely the Secret Service. Mitleer goes on to explain

that there would be multiple assassins when using the word, 'We' when describing the assassination plot. He was eluding to the existence of a patsy when describing a man with a high-powered rifle would be picked up within hours of the assassination to throw the public off.

So, who killed Kennedy? The answer is ironically straightforward. When examining the historical analysis of conspiracy theorists, regarding the JFK assassination we will find that nearly every group you could imagine, was considered to be involved; including The Mafia, The Jesuit Catholic Church, the Vatican, The CIA, The Secret Service, and secret societies. All of these groups, at that time through the present day, are components of the Deep State. Although it may become easy to be overwhelmed with small details like this, however when put into perspective, the answer becomes quite simple. Many people and many different groups working together as one machine, who were heavily financed, meticulous planned the JFK assassination. Kennedy's assassins were a network of Deep State conspirators. It even went as far as involving the Houston mayor, at the time, in 1963, who persuaded the Secret Service to change Kennedy's motorcade route to be rerouted through Elm Street, adjacent to the depository and open storm drains.

The Shot from Below Theory, which forensic analysis of Kennedys head wounds proves that the fatal bullet exited the top of the back of his head, which means he was shot from below, which is also consistent with the Grassy Knoll Theory; although this theory comes close to explaining the fatal shot fired from below, to be more precise John F Kennedys fatal shot, came from the Elm Street storm drain. This idea is also consistent with the belief that he was also shot multiple times by multiple assassins, some being members of his secret service. This explains the multiple gunshot wounds to JFK's head, most notably the single gunshot (of multiple gunshots), which under audio forensics analysis demonstrates an echo, differentiating it from the other shots fired.

In the sixties, one could crawl or walk through a sewer system, quite easily by simply lifting a manhole cover and walk through it with a flashlight and heading down a street (Elm Street) unseen. This was how one of the multiple killers was able to fire the fatal shot killing Kennedy. It would be easy to dismiss this as speculation, if not for the video and audio analysis of the JFK assignation [assassination]. The audio is readily available on the internet, where you can clearly hear one of the shots echoing as the others did not.

Oswald, of course, was not the lone gunman but instead was working the CIA, then framed by them. The Deep state had their fall guy, and 'patsy' ordered (using some unknown blackmail tactic) to be situated inside the depository building. The Deep State positioned him there, not to kill JFK, but as Mitleer stated, 'they will pick somebody up within hours afterward, anything like that would happen just to throw the public off.' John F Kennedy's head wound exited the top left side part of his skull. The storm sewer assassin placed himself to fire the fatal shot from the right passenger side of Kennedy's motorcade, on Elm Street; from the storm sewer. Since there were multiple shooters, they had a backup system in place.

This is how the Deep State operates, with its many components and many groups, with many people organizing an assassination plot containing many assassins; the result, as the Deep State fully understood, would always be a confused public reaction (producing conspiracy theories), and the operation would nearly always be a complete one. The cover-up was easy. The hard part, of course, was having their scapegoat in place, with so many components actively financed and working in tandem, with deliberate planning, months in advance. It is no coincidence that with so many agencies involved, The Deep State was able to get away with such a horrible and tragic murder. The Deep State continues to operate this way, it always has and always will, as long as there is enough money and evil to go around.

George Bush Senior was working at the CIA at the time of the JFK assignation. He also lived in Houston where he worked for an offshore oil company. He was purported positively identified in photographs and by eyewitnesses as being seen at the scene of the crime. J Edgar Hoover sent a note to the FBI inquiring about a George Bush, and his involvement with the JFK assignation. George Bush Senior denied the existence of any involvement claiming he did not work for the CIA during the JFK assassination citing documentation showing another George Bush who was just a paper shuffling clerk, also working for the CIA during the Kennedy assassination. The other George Bush was used as a Deep State prop to diffuse the legitimacy of the accusation further. This is also known as the story of two George Bush's.

Operation Zapata was CIA code for 'The Bay of Pigs,' subverted by the CIA who notified Castro of the Kennedys secret plot to invade Cuba; allowing 1,500 trained CIA Cuban Exiles to be arrested, captured and imprisoned. Jeopardizing the entire military operation and forever besmirching Kennedy's name and intentionally bungling The Bay of Pigs. CIA Code for the 'Bay of Pigs' was 'Zapata,' and is significant because it was also the name the offshore oil company George Bush Senior worked for named,' Zapata Offshore Oil Company'! The reason why the Deep State left so many clues was the idea had anyone put all of these pieces together must be a conspiracy theorist, to be quickly dispelled and denounced in an effort to never allow uncovering what atrocities the

Deep State has committed. Although George Bush Sr. claims he was not working in the CIA at the time of the Kennedy assassination, he was indeed working for the CIA then, and responsible for hiring every one of the 1,500 CIA recruits for the Cuban exiled Army who invaded the Bay of Pigs.

[handwritten: Holy Sheet]

George Bush Sr was also the director of the former Warren Commission investigating the JFK assassination. It bears mentioning that George Bush Senior also officially formed the New World Order with Bill Clinton and George Wallace in 1982. The Deep State are communists who do not want prosperity for our nation; instead they have a New World agenda which directly opposes our traditional Capitalist one. Transcripts of Nixon's 'White House Watergate Tapes' reveals Nixon's use of codenames 'Cubans' and 'Texans' when referring to Bush, Mosbacher, and Baker, (Nixon's partners and Fundraisers) linking both Bush and Nixon to the JFK assassination. Nixon's Watergate tapes also show that when Nixon described JFK's assassination, he used the code phrase 'Bay of Pigs'!

"Each of us has the hope to build a New World Order."

– Richard Nixon, February 1972

According to JFK's secretary, Mrs. Lincoln, John F Kennedy, and Robert Kennedy argued incessantly about what to do about Johnson's plot to expose Kennedy's lady friends. The solution JFK and RFK came up with is by now no longer a mystery; John F Kennedy would agree to submit to Johnsons Deep State blackmail, by making LBJ his Vice President.

After President Kennedy's death, Jacqueline Kennedy inquired to know who was behind the conspiracy to kill her husband and was very specific about wanting a neutral third-party, not the Deep State agencies involved in her private investigation. Jacqueline Kennedy privately asked both the Soviet government and French government to investigate who was behind the Kennedy assignation, both Governments reported back to her with the same report, Lyndon Baines Johnson was at the highest level of the plot to assassinate John F. Kennedy.

On November 21, 1963, LBJ told his mistress:

"Those Sons of Bitches will never embarrass me again. That's not a threat. That's a promise."

- Lyndon B. Johnson, November 21, 1963

The very next day, President John F Kennedy was dead.

JFK & THE FEDERAL RESERVE

53 | HISTORY OF THE DEEP STATE

On June 4, 1963, unknown Presidential decree, Executive Order 11110, was signed with authority to strip the Rothschild Bank of its power to loan money to the United States Federal Government at interest. President Kennedy declared that the privately-owned Rothschild Federal Reserve Bank would soon be out of business.

When President John Fitzgerald Kennedy signed this Order, it returned to the United States federal government, specifically the Treasury Department, the Constitutional power to create and issue currency - money – without going through the privately-owned Rothschild Federal Reserve Bank.

If you don't want to anger the Deep State, then don't screw with their money. Again, every President who has meddled with our foreign-owned banking system, whether it was the First Bank of the U.S., The Second

Bank of the U.S. or The Federal Reserve; was either assassinated or had an attempted assassination against them. Jackson, Garfield, Lincoln, and Kennedy all meddled with the Deep State financed Rosicrucian Banking system and paid the price for doing it.

I will go over the particulars of each one of these Presidents brazen stance against Deep State money in a later chapter (The Rosicrucian Banking System). For now, we will refocus our attention on John F Kennedy. It is essential to begin with the understanding that the United States banking system, since its Inception in 1776 all of our Banks have been and currently are not federally owned banking property. Instead, the Federal Reserve through present day is still a privately-owned conglomeration of foreign communists and private Deep State investors. John F Kennedy was well a well-educated President, with a vast understanding of economics exemplified in his understanding of the relationship between tax cuts, economic growth, and stimulation; creating a broad economic base, by lifting the burden of over taxation, a higher tax, becomes unnecessary; as expansion continues economically.

President John F Kennedy was also very well aware of the immediate presence of a Deep State. Evidence for this lies in the fact that Lyndon Baines Johnson, Kennedy's Vice President was given the position of vice presidency through blackmail, infiltrating his way into Government and eventually to become President. LBJ did this by blackmailing JFK with the threat that either Kennedy would give him Vice Presidency or Johnson would go public with the information which he gained from the CIA of John F Kennedy's long history of affairs with various women outside of his marriage with Jacqueline Kennedy. This scandal, of course, if it were to get out, would ruin JFK politically, especially in late 1961; when scandalous accusations like those against

Kennedy would ruin a man politically, financially and his reputation permanently. It would also ruin any chance he would hope to have in being reelected.

Incidentally, Kennedy only narrowly defeated Johnson in the 1961 presidential race. Johnson was effectively a mole for the Deep State, being blackmailed; in this way, Kennedy fully understood the corruption that happens at that level of government. Also, you must keep in mind John F Kennedy's father, Joe Kennedy, was indeed the most powerful member of all secret societies, Illuminati, Freemasons, Knights of Malta, The Pilgrim Society, and all secret societies. John Kennedy was no stranger to the corruption of the Deep State. He went going into the Oval Office with a complete understanding of the problems he would face and the dangerous, challenges and conflicts he would encounter with The Deep State. Kennedy, armed with this knowledge, appointed his brother, someone whom you could trust unequivocally as his Attorney

General. By then, The Department of Justice, which was estimated in the Smoot report of 1961, that Communists infiltrated the entire Department of Justice. Kennedy's decision to appoint his brother as Attorney General of the United States in his administration was no coincidence. It was a calculated defense against what was to come, he foresaw his battles with the Deep state and moreover, it was also further evidence that he was fully aware of the Deep State, when he privately signed executive order 11110, which explicitly gave The U.S. Treasury Department the authority to issue Silver Certificates or, also known as United States Notes; which were backed by silver and silver bullion. Prior to 1963 the two and five-dollar bill denominations had the words 'Federal Reserve Note' written at the top of each one of these bills; but by the summer of 1963 the Federal Reserve Note, which was not backed by anything of intrinsic value, instead backed by the assurance that foreign investors had the ability to keep the money invested in the Federal Reserve. When backing our currency with silver, President John F Kennedy eliminated the need for private and foreign Deep State investors. Foreign investors would not have any sway or influence over our economy under Kennedys Silver Bullion backed currency. In effect, he was essentially killing all prior Investments and one of the major components of the Deep state overnight. With the $2 note and $5 note both in circulation in 1963, already, an estimated 6 million dollars' worth of these notes amounted to approximately 4 billion dollars' worth of United States Notes.

Kennedy's United States Notes, had they been brought into full circulation, would have given the United States the ability to pay back its debt, due to the fact that Kennedy's United States notes backed by silver and obviated the need to pay back interest to foreign investor backed Federal Reserve notes; which charged interest. It is estimated that the amount of elimination of Interest accrued, even throughout the Obama administration, would have quickly been paid off, just by eliminating the interest charged by private Federal Reserve Banks anyone

HISTORY OF THE DEEP STATE

living through the summer of 1963, with money in their pocket pockets ($5 or $2 bills) were slowly but surely where becoming aware, that a comparison of $2 and $5 notes would reveal one displaying the words 'Federal Reserve Note', which was not backed by silver, and another displaying the words 'United States Note'. The public was rapidly becoming aware that' something Insidious was taking place inside our government. Also, The Federal Reserve Seal was removed along with any Illuminati symbolism in the 'United States Note.' The Kennedy $2 and $5-dollar notes displayed a red color. In 1963 two completely different currencies, (or notes) were both printed by The US Department Treasury Department. Some noticed the distinction between the two notes and referred to the 'Federal Reserve Note' as 'fake money' and Kennedy's note as 'real money' backed by silver.

As people began to take notice, this became a problem for the Deep State for obvious reasons. The public outcry would demand an explanation and could expose the Deep state corruption. This was of course not their only problem. Their biggest problem for them, was The President stripping the money from these privately owned foreign banking systems and the interest and the influence they had over United States currency. A solution was essential for the Deep state, and as they have done with former Presidents who medaled with their finances, decided the solution would be the assassination of John F Kennedy. The Treasury Department was also printing tens, and Twenty Silver Certificate notes just before Kennedy's assassination. Although these notes never went into circulation, had the Deep State not assassinated President John F Kennedy; twos, fives, twenties, hundreds, and thousand-dollar notes all would have been silver certificates, altogether eliminating the Deep States interest and investments into our economy. Our economy would have easily been 5 to 10 times what it currently is today, had Kennedy silver certificates remained in circulation. The same man who had ordered the assassination of JFK, within just months into his Presidency, LBJ reversed Kennedy's 11110 executive order, and replaced it with executive order 10289, removing Kennedy's United States note from circulation as U.S. currency and bringing back the Federal Reserve Notes for foreign investors. No President would ever dare meddle with Americas Foreign-backed Deep State currency again.

CHAPTER THREE
THE DEEP STATE ILLUMINATI

On May 1st, 1776 the 'Order of the Illuminati', or The Illuminati of Bavaria A.K.A. 'The Ancient and Illuminated Seers of Bavaria.' The Order of the Illuminati was formed in the city of Ingolstadt, within the southern German aristocracy of Bavaria; by a former practicing Jew, Jesuit-trained Priest, and law professor at the University of Bavaria, Adam Weishaupt. Incidentally, this was not his real name; Rather, this was also a ploy to deceive Germans subconsciously. When one breaks down the name Adam Weishaupt, we get Adam, (The first man in creation) Weis, (meaning knowledge and wisdom, in German) and Haupt (meaning leader, in German). Adam was also a former 33rd degree Free Mason, who decided to push the barriers of evil and satanic practices, which were limited and restricted within the Masonic traditions; by revealing Masonic secrets and utilizing Islamic Mysticism (Sufism).

The date which was chosen for the official formation of the Illuminati, May 1st is no coincidence. As has already been eluded to, May 1st is the first day of the Pagan Summer Solstice, a tradition dating back thousands of years, celebrated by the ancient Greeks and Roman Empire. May 1st is also 'Witches Day' and is still celebrated today, throughout Europe and privately in the United States by occultists and high-ranking Illuminatus members. Even more significantly, it is exactly 66 days ahead of the Fourth of July.

The origin of the word 'Illuminati' comes from the Gnostic dichotomy between light and darkness. Which also explains the symbolism between the date of Pagan Summer Solstice (66 days before July 4th, 1776) and the traditionally Christian Summer Solstice on June 21st (13 days before the July 4th, 1776), as it relates to our Nations Declaration of Independence.

In order to entice new members into this secret society it was incredibly important for them to have a stated objective of being a seemly good, philanthropic, harmless and even helpful in the pursuit of a better and more globalized world:

"To stimulate a human and sociable vision: Support virtue where it may be threatened or oppressed by vice; to promote the progress of merit worth people and foster the benefit of those deprived of education."

- Adam Weishaupt

HISTORY OF THE DEEP STATE

Thomas Jefferson called recalled Illuminati founder Adam Weishaupt to be "a harmless philanthropist." Adam Weishaupt's sales pitch, when making phony claims that the Illuminati was simply a 'harmless Secret Society' was bought into by Thomas Jefferson himself. Although the reason for this is unclear, it is very likely that as a lower level Illuminist, Jefferson was deliberately fooled as most lower lever members were; and not given a complete understanding of The Deep State Illuminists real intentions, motivations, and objectives. Jefferson regarding Weishaupt:

"Weishaupt believes that to promote this perfection of the human character was the object of Jesus Christ. That his intention was simply to reinstate natural religion, & by diffusing the light of his morality, to teach us to govern ourselves. His precepts are the love of

God & love of our neighbor. And by teaching innocence of conduct, he expected to place men in their natural state of liberty & equality. He says, no one ever laid a surer foundation for liberty than our grand master, Jesus of Nazareth. He believes the Freemasons were originally possessed of the true principles & objects of Christianity, & have still preserved some of them by tradition, but much disfigured. The means he proposes to effect this improvement of human nature are "to enlighten men, to correct their morals & inspire them with benevolence. Secure of our success, sais he, we abstain from violent commotions. To have foreseen, the happiness of posterity & to have prepared it by irreproachable means suffices for our felicity. The tranquility of our consciences is not troubled by the reproach of aiming at the ruin or

67 | HISTORY OF THE DEEP STATE

overthrow of states or thrones. As Weishaupt lived under the tyranny of a despot & priests, he knew that caution was necessary even in spreading information, & the principles of pure morality. He proposed, therefore, to lead the Freemasons to adopt this object & to make the objects of their institution the diffusion of science & virtue. He proposed to initiate new members into his body by gradations proportioned to his fears of the thunderbolts of tyranny. This has given an air of mystery to his views, was the foundation of his banishment, the subversion of the Masonic order, & is the colour for the ravings against him of Robinson, Barruel & Morse, whose real fears are that the craft would be endangered by the spreading of information, reason, & natural morality among men. This subject being new to me, I have imagined that if it be so to you also, you may receive the same satisfaction in seeing, which I have had in forming the analysis of it: & I believe you will think with me that if Weishaupt had written here, where no secrecy is necessary in our endeavors to render men wise & virtuous, he would not have thought of any secret machinery for that purpose. As Godwin, if he had written in Germany, might probably also have thought secrecy & mysticism prudent. I will say nothing to you on the late revolution of France, which is painfully interesting. Perhaps when we know more of the circumstances which gave rise to it, & the direction it will take, Buonaparte, its chief organ, may stand in a better light than at present. I am with great esteem, dear sir, your affectionate friend."

- Thomas Jefferson to James Madison, 1/31/1800

The stated objective, when initiating recruits is far different from their true objective, which isn't revealed until every Illuminati rite is complete, as stated in

'The Illuminati Oath':

"An illusion it will be, so large, so vast it will escape their perception. Those who will see it will be thought of as insane. We will create separate fronts to prevent them from seeing the connection between us. We will behave as if we are not connected to keep the illusion alive. Our goal will be accomplished one drop at a time to never bring suspicion upon ourselves. This will also prevent them from seeing the changes as they occur.

We will always stand above the relative field of their experience for we know the secrets of the absolute. We will work together always and will remain bound by blood and secrecy. Death will come to he who speaks.

'We will keep their lifespan short and their minds weak while pretending to do the opposite.' We will use our knowledge of science and technology in subtle ways, so they will never see what is happening. We will use soft metals, aging accelerators and sedatives in food and water, also in the air. They will be blanketed by poisons everywhere they turn.

The soft metals will cause them to lose their minds. We will promise to find a cure from our many fronts, yet we will feed them more poison. The poisons will be absorbed through their skin and mouths; they will destroy their minds and reproductive systems. From all this, their children will be born dead, and we will conceal this information.

Processed foods?

The poisons will be hidden in everything that surrounds them, in what they drink, eat, breathe and wear. We must be ingenious in dispensing the poisons for they can see far. We will teach them that the poisons are good, with fun images and musical tones. Those

HISTORY OF THE DEEP STATE

they look up to will help. We will enlist them to push our poisons. They will see our products being used in film and will grow accustomed to them and will never know their true effect.' When they give birth, we will inject poisons into the blood of their children and convince them it is for their help. We will start early on, when their minds are young, we will target their children with what children love most, sweet things. When their teeth decay we will fill them with metals that will kill their mind and steal their future. When their ability to learn has been affected, we will create medicine that will make them sicker and cause other diseases for which we will create more medicine yet. We will render them docile and weak before us by our power. They will grow depressed, slow and obese, and when they come to us for help, we will give them more poison. We will focus their attention toward money and material goods so they many never connect with their inner self. We will distract them with fornication, external pleasures and games so they may never be one with the oneness of it all. Their minds will belong to us, and they will do as we say. If they refuse, we shall find ways to implement mind-altering technology into their lives. We will use fear as our weapon. We will establish their governments and establish opposites within. We will own both sides. We will always hide our objective but carry out our plan. They will perform the labor for us, and we shall prosper from their toil.

'Our families will never mix with theirs. Our blood must be pure always, for it is the way.' We will make them kill each other when it suits us. We will keep them separated from the oneness through dogma and religion. We will control all aspects of their lives and tell them what to think and how.

'We will guide them kindly and gently letting them think they are guiding themselves.'

We will foment animosity between them through our factions. When a light shall shine among them, we shall extinguish it by ridicule, or death, whichever suits us best. We will make them rip each other's hearts apart and kill their children. We will

73 | HISTORY OF THE DEEP STATE

accomplish this by using hate as our ally, anger as our friend. The hate will blind them totally, and never shall they see that from their conflicts we emerge as their rulers.

They will be busy killing each other. They will bathe in their blood and kill their neighbors for as long as we see fit. We will benefit greatly from this, for they will not see us, for they cannot see us. We will continue to prosper from their wars and their deaths. We shall repeat this over and over until our ultimate goal is accomplished. We will continue to make them live in fear and anger though images and sounds. We will use all the tools we have to accomplish this. The tools will be provided by their labor. We will make them hate themselves and their neighbors. We will always hide the divine truth from them, that we are all one. This they must never know! They must never know that color is an illusion, they must always think they are not equal. Drop by drop, drop by drop we will advance our goal. 'We will take over their land, resources and wealth to exercise total control over them.'

We will deceive them into accepting laws that will steal the little freedom they will have.' We will establish a money system that will imprison them forever, keeping them and their children in debt'. When they shall ban together, we shall accuse them of crimes and present a different story to the world for we shall own all the media. We will use our media to control the flow of information and their sentiment in our favor. When they shall rise against us, we will crush them like insects, for they are less than that. They will be helpless to do anything for they will have no weapons.

We will recruit some of their own to carry out our plans, we will promise them eternal life, but eternal life they will never have for they are not of us. The recruits will be called "initiates" and will be indoctrinated to believe false rites of passage to higher realms. Members of these groups will think they are one with us never knowing the truth.

They must never learn this truth for they will turn against us. For their work, they will be rewarded with earthly things and great titles,

75 | HISTORY OF THE DEEP STATE

but never will they become immortal and join us, never will they receive the light and travel the stars. They will never reach the higher realms, for the killing of their kind will prevent passage to the realm of enlightenment. This they will never know.

The truth will be hidden in their face, so close they will not be able to focus on it until it's too late. Oh yes, so grand the illusion of freedom will be, that they will never know they are our slaves.

'When all is in place, the reality we will have created for them will own them. This reality will be their prison.' They will live in self-delusion. When our goal is accomplished a new era of domination will begin. Their beliefs will bind Their minds, the beliefs we have established from time immemorial.

But if they ever find out they are our equal, we shall perish then. This they must never know. If they ever find out that together they can vanquish us, they will take action. They must never, ever find out what we have done, for if they do, we shall have no place to run,

HISTORY OF THE DEEP STATE

for it will be easy to see who we are once the veil has fallen. Our actions will have revealed who we are, and they will hunt us down, and no person shall shelter us.

This is the secret covenant by which we shall live the rest of our present and future lives, for this reality will transcend many generations and life spans. Blood, our blood seal this covenant. We, the ones who from heaven to earth came. This covenant must never be known to exist.

It must never be written or spoken of for if it is, the consciousness it will spawn will release the fury of the Prime Creator upon us and we shall be cast to the depths from whence we came and remain there until the end time of infinity itself."

– Unknown Illuminatus

Once the members are entirely indoctrinated with the illusion of an 'Innocuous Secret Society,' whose stated goal was the attainment of wisdom, and the oath is taken; their true stated goals are then revealed:

↓ = One World Order or Globalism

I. Eradication of all Governments (Overthrowing the State)

II. Eradication of inheritance (Control over wealth and monetary distribution)

III. Eradication of property rights (Deep State Quasi-Communism)

IV. Eradication of Nationalism and Patriotism (Disbanding of Countries)

V. Population reduction (Rise of a New World Elitism)

VI. Eradication of religion (Satanism)

VII. Eradication of family (Secular Culture)

VIII. The formation of a New World Government (New World Order or a 'Deep State')

THE AMERICAN REVOLUTION & THE DEEP STATE

Before briefly touching on the 13 Illuminati families, and their prominence in Government; It should by now be crystal clear that the people at the bottom are not typically of these 13 Illuminati families. They are the sheep, never coming to a complete understanding of what lies at the top of this pyramidal system. Those of the bloodline, however, are indoctrinated early on, but this also does not seem to allow them to inherit the right to a complete understanding of their mission. It does appear that if they are genuinely interested, are afforded an unfettered path to gain nearly anything they desire; without any constraint of the law, being protected, fostered, and sheltered by the family. Their mission of a one world Government of elites, population control,

HISTORY OF THE DEEP STATE

breakdown of the family and religion/morality etcetera, is not for them; but for the enemy.

(handwritten: Example John Brennan)

The Deep State may seem to be a phenomenon, that only recently took shape during the Obama administration. While it is true that Obama has doubled up the infiltration process by embedding more agents inside these various 'Intelligence Agencies,' history shows that during the 1920's the Rockefeller family fully infiltrated 'Communists' into these agencies by design; and were very successful in doing so. These Communists, as they were referred to by Joseph McCarthy, one could easily dismiss this notion altogether as a being out of place and from different time and era. After all, we're not in a Cold War, or fighting Communists anymore, are we? We never were, at least not externally. The fight against Communism paradoxically has always only been, for the most part, an internal one. The names have changed, but the players have always had the same agenda. American patriots used to be straight shooters, this is the heart of who we are, and as Americans, we must never forget how vital this is in defining our American spirit. We started by calling the enemy out by name, exactly as they were, Communists; but even then, the idea was quickly impugned, and with the help of Main Stream Media, acedia [academia], mind control, mob hypnotism, and the controlled misuse of Government leaders of words; the word 'Communism' has effectively been taken out of fashionable circulation and replaced by innocuous euphemisms.

First, they fancied themselves as, 'Leftists,' then 'Liberals,' then 'Progressives' then 'Libertarians.' They're all still Communists with the same 'Communist' agenda. Then you'll say OK; it started in the 20's, that's not so bad. The infiltration of Communism in the 20's was just the second wave of a broader Deep State infiltration. There are in fact three waves, and they deepen as they go. We are living in the age of the third wave of Deep State invasion.

The first wave of the Deep State began a very long time ago. It began where its tentacles didn't take root until 1776. Adam Weishaupt vision of a New World Order was only discovered either by sheer coincidence or by the hand of God. As the story goes, as the Electoral of Bavaria (essentially a type of King) began to take notice of the Order of Illuminati's practices inside Masonic Temples, (Masonry was also infiltrated, forming a Secret Society embedded inside another) raided Masonic temples across Bavaria. This Electoral of Bavaria passed laws, soon prohibiting every kind of secret meeting. Even Free Masonic meetings, since they were by then primarily overrun by the Illuminati was no exception to this new law; arresting any who were caught practicing Illuminati rites, with the intention to eradicate their evil from the culture. As these raids were conducted, on July 10th, 1785, a personal friend of Weishaupt's, being aware of the danger to their Secret Society, took off on horse, fleeing with the secret papers containing the true plot and agenda of the Illuminati of world domination.

As he rode into the night, a storm was brewing and as strange as it may seem, he was, in fact, struck dead by lighting, while in route to France. His scorched body, with the secret Order of the Illuminati doctrine documents laying with him, still intact. The Bavarian authorities found him dead, seizing all the secret documents hidden inside his boot. After discovering Weishaupt plan to overthrow the Governments of the world through a diabolical scheme, of internal invasion (The Deep State manifesto) written in his handwriting, The Deep States agenda was exposed. Weishaupt was immediately expelled from the Bavarian University and forever banished from his Country. Before going underground into hiding, Weishaupt swore to the authorities of Bavaria that he would come back ten times more powerful.

While his statement may have seemed like a grandiose display of denial in being defeated,

83 | HISTORY OF THE DEEP STATE

Weishaupt was making a statement in fact. His fomentation of the French Revolution, being fully funded through the Rothchild's global enterprise (amounting to complete control of virtually all of the money in Europe) was already underway.

Over a relatively short span of time, (1771 through 1785) the order of the Illuminati and its Deep State agenda to topple Governments around the globe, spread like wildfire throughout Europe. Although the agenda was nearly revealed to the world, he managed to publish a new pronouncement of a set of peaceful objectives and fooled the world yet again. Adam feigned returning to his roots as a Jesuit Priest, forever giving up the practices of the Illuminati. With this proclamation to the world and going entirely underground, he gained his reputation for being a God-fearing, philanthropic purest back.

The messenger who was struck and killed by lighting had, in fact, a two-pronged mission. Although Weishaupt inner circle were fleeing Bavaria, Weishaupt currier was also in route to France; with the instructions on exactly how to overthrow the "Nation State.' The message was intended for Maximilien Robespierre; a self-proclaimed advocate for the compassion of the poor, solving the 18th century's French version of food and income inequality, and opposition to the death penalty. Robespierre intentions were quite the opposite, feigning all of these philanthropic ideologies to gain political power, to foment, then launch a 'French Revolution.'

You see, Robespierre was not Philanthropic at all; he was also an Illuminatus and was merely practicing the deceptive Illuminati tenants outlined by Adam Weishaupt. The French Revolutionary War was not a revolution undertaken by the bourgeoisie people of France revolting against their French King, as history falsely records. In truth, it was the first calculated Deep State coup d'état. Weishaupt fomented, calculated, and planned a coup d'état disguised as a 'Peoples Uprising Revolution,' similarly utilizing the same philanthropic tactics the left imitates today, in the United States, to inflame an illusion of a hostile and violent people, ready for war.

The French revolution was in truth, just a hired group of assassins who were carrying out the orders of The Illuminati to overthrow a Nation State, (Church and State) with a Deep State.

"I trust that your future Acquaintance with the Executive of the State will evince to you that among their faults is not to be counted a want of disposition to second the Views of the Commander against our common Enemy. We are too much interested in the present Scene and have too much at Stake to leave a doubt on that Head. Mild Laws, a People not used to war and prompt obedience, a want of the Provisions of War and means of procuring them render our orders often ineffectual, oblige us to temporize and when we cannot accomplish an object in one way to attempt it in another. Your knowledge of the Circumstances with a temper accommodated to them ensure me your Cooperation in the

best way we can when we shall not be able to pursue the Way we would wish.

I still hope you will find our Preparations not far short of the Information I took the Liberty of giving you in my Letter of the 8th. instant. I shall be very happy to receive your freest Applications for whatever may be necessary for the Public Service, and to convince you of our Disposition to promote it as far as the abilities of the State and Powers of the Executive will enable us; and have the Honour to be with the Highest Esteem & Respect Sir Your, &c."

- Thomas Jefferson to Lafayette, March 10th. 1781

Jefferson's open and frequent correspondence was undoubtedly necessary to maintain an ongoing plan to receive aid, military force, and monies from the French to defeat the British Empire. There is no question, that without the help of the French Government, (Militarily and financially) we did not stand a fighting chance in defeating the British Redcoat Army. Without working together with the French, America would have lost the Revolutionary War. Americans had the spirit and the tactical know how but did not have the superior weaponry as the British Redcoats did nor the military budget to sustain us to victory given to us by the French. But why were they so willing to go out of their way to help us fight such an expensive War? Was it merely because we had a familiar foe, The British? This is an unlikely solitary incentive for the French to help us so often, and for such a protracted period of time.

In order to explain the true motivation of the French and their unusual eagerness to do partake in our American Revolutionary War begins with the story of a man also known as 'The Hero of Two Worlds', Marquis De Lafayette. Lafayette nickname was given to him because he was given most of the credit for the success of two major revolutions, the French and American Revolutions. While the American Revolution was an undeniable fight for freedom from the oppression of the British Monarchy, the 'French Revolution' was hardly a war; it was an organized coup d'état that was accomplished in less than 24 hours and the simplicity of its operation, leaves an honest observer wondering if there wasn't more to the story.

The true story of Marquis De Lafayette is somewhat disturbing but unveils the mystery behind of the true origin of the Deep State.

Marquis De Lafayette was called upon by General George Washington for assistance in fighting the greatest superpower at the time, The British Empire. France joined forces with The United States in the American Revolutionary War in 1779, after the Battle of Saratoga. Before they Naval assistance, The U.S. was losing virtually every battle with the British. but what prompted them to come to our assistance so quickly, and without anything in return?

HISTORY OF THE DEEP STATE

Before Lafayette came to America during the Revolutionary War, Marquis was a lobbyist for America and France. Lobbyists, of course, don't work for free. Lafayette was related to the Du Pont Illuminati family and was a high-ranking Illuminatus; even before The Order of the Illuminati was recognized on May 1st, 1776. It is well documented in history prior to his involvement in the American Revolutionary War that he held regular meetings with none other than Adam Weishaupt himself, between 1773 and 1779. Moreover, Weishaupt traveled from Germany to France specifically to speak with Lafayette. These meetings were known to the public and what was discussed was done inside Masonic Temples where Illuminati Secret Societies were held inside. The same message of subversion and infiltration of a Deep State that was passed onto Maximilien Robespierre for the French Revolutionary War was also given, by Weishaupt to Lafayette. Weishaupt planned the overthrow of The French Monarchy, and with the American Government; he saw a way to exploit a weakness in a failing American Revolution.

The diabolical plot to subvert America and eventually overthrow its 'Church and State' was planned years in advance, except with America all eight of Weishaupt's methods to destroy Governments from within were implemented for the long haul. It's no coincidence that the Order of the Illuminati was founded on May 1st, 1776 and the Declaration of Independence was exactly 66 days later on July 4th, 1776; With Lafayette in place as the unofficial ambassador between Thomas Jefferson and Weishaupt. Unbeknown to Jefferson, who was enamored with a new form of wisdom and enlightenment officially becoming an Order, An American Deep State was formed.

CHAPTER FOUR
ANCIENT SYMBOLISM

When we talk about ancient symbolism, we'd be remiss not to start from the beginning of time; since the Illuminati is just an offshoot of Free Masonry or what I would call 'Radical Free-Masonry'. They too feel they are doing good in some demented and warped way. In their quest for wisdom, both the Masons and the Illuminati have to study God to understand evil. Their quest isn't a journey to find wisdom; it's a journey to find pure evil. Sadly, they don't even know what they're dabbling in. Since there are no books directly written by Satan, the Bible and Torah are the only places they can collect data, to reverse engineer God.

Let's start with what is at the foundation of an old Jewish offshoot sect of Judaism, called the 'Kabbalists' or people that study the Kabbala. Judaism, in its pure practice, has nothing to do with any of these Satanic practices. Unfortunately, over time mankind will find a way to pervert nearly anything that was once good; and although the Kabbala has taken and examined many mathematical anomalies to reveal strange patterns found in shapes, numbers, dates, times and Greek text, it will never lead to enlightenment.

From the Kabbala, the natural progression is to look into pagan religions; Ancient Roman Gods, Babylonian deities, Greek mythology, Hinduism, and even Yoga. Secret Societies study all of these things along with the Bible. Many of them probably know the Bible better than most theologians. Since they are not permitted to discuss religion, you will probably never know that fact first hand.

The bottom line is these people have always been aristocrats, Nobles, and elites, traditionally. The common man on the street is below them and doesn't deserve the fruits of what they stole from legitimate 'wise men.' Weishaupt took Free Masonry as far as it could go but put a caveat in it. Why let members decide what is right or wrong, as the Masons seem to do, especially in the lower degrees; when you can spread it like wildfire by enticing people with the appeal of something pure and Christ-like? After all, they're smart enough to understand you can't get anyone onboard by directly telling the world about a secret plot to overthrow all governments, a one world Government, dismantling the family, abolishing religion altogether, and becoming a Satan Worshipper. Only a fool would sign up for something like that. The key to getting so many members is based on a simple principle. There are a lot of people who hate God but would love some wisdom!

Gnostic is their favorite word, which Webster's Dictionary defines as: 'the thought and practice especially of various cults of late pre-Christian and early Christian centuries distinguished by the conviction that matter is evil, and that emancipation comes through gnosis.' Interesting that this is how these Secret Societies describe the essence of their

95 | HISTORY OF THE DEEP STATE

teachings because they are obsessed with matter, objects and the like. The letter 'G' can be found all over any Masonic temple or lodge. That's what it stands for, Gnostic.

Weishaupt never showed his face to his cult followers, only to the closest members in his innermost circle. This is the essence of mysticism, its mystery. The father of the Deep State took something already extraordinarily subtle and made it even more subtle. Instead of using secret temples shrouded in mysterious hieroglyphics and strange symbols to get recruits, why not forgo that, and lure the masses in with a stated promise of wisdom and benevolence for all mankind?!

Why not infiltrate and seize control over all Governments, industry, companies, property rights, music, the arts, and popular culture; then proudly advertise and display their mystical symbols on every Government flag,

moniker, family crest, corporate sign, and last but not least, money and currency itself. Where everyone can notice the evil subtly, subconsciously luring them in by the droves, on the broadest scale imaginable?! Here we are, nearly two hundred and fifty years later,

97 | HISTORY OF THE DEEP STATE

where we can't go even a few minutes without being bombarded with their imagery everywhere we look. Every sign, every flag, every currency, spanning the globe you cannot escape it. Mind control, mob hypnosis and subliminal cues were not a foreign concept to Weishaupt, because today they are ubiquitous. We're immersed in Satanic hypnosis.

This brings us to the ever-present, United States, one-dollar bill. When examining the

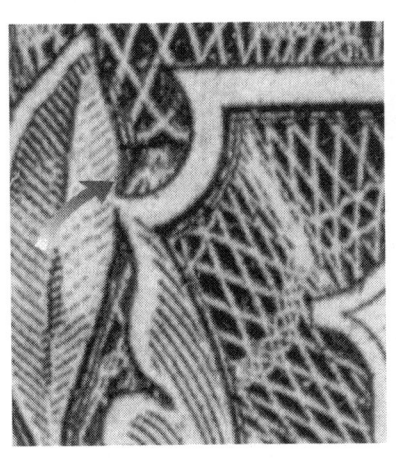

one-dollar bill today, with all of its strange symbols and hidden meanings; It is necessary, to begin with a man named Haym Solomon. Although history has virtually omitted the accurate account of Solomon's life, being the most significant man in United States history, it begs the question, why?

The unseemly and sinister plot against the United States, which he engaged in, explains precisely why.
Haym Solomon immigrated to the United States in 1772, where he founded a brokerage business in New York City.

While there are no accounts of Haym practicing Judaism, instead we know from a book entitled '10 Thousand Famous Freemasons' that he was a practicing Free Mason and high-ranking Illuminatus and cited as being a paymaster, (an official who pays troops or workers) He was a legal Polish Immigrant situating himself in Philadelphia. During the winter of 1772, Haym Solomon met with General Washington to find them in a state of complete disarray and nearly ready surrender to the British. Washington's ragtag army being without uniforms and depleted of

HISTORY OF THE DEEP STATE

military resources; many of them without shoes.

Being in the most in the desperate and dire of circumstances, Washington had no choice but to secretly agree to be financed by an unknown Jewish banker and representative of the Rothschilds foreign banking system. Solomon was fully backed by prominent Rothchild owned investors and bankers from Holland, France and throughout Europe. He successfully brokered deals between the Rothchild's and The United States with George Washington, Jefferson, Adams and the committee of Franklin to help finance The American Revolutionary War. Haym Salomon worked with General Layfette to obtain and negotiate all the wartime subsides and money necessary to seal the

Deep State deal; without being blackmailed and bribed, General Washington and our brave American troops would have lost the American Revolution.

"A holy war will now begin on America, and when it is ended America will be supposedly the citadel of freedom, but her millions will unknowingly be loyal subjects to the Crown. Your churches will be used to teach the Jew's religion, and in less than two hundred years the whole nation will be working for divine world government. That government that they believe to be divine will be the British Empire. All religions will be permeated with Judaism without even being noticed by the masses, and they will all be under the invisible all-seeing eye of the Grand Architect of Freemasonry."

- British General Cornwallis, 1781

Haym continued his Deep State entrapment through 1785, and when the US Treasury was nearly depleted, he advanced all need money to Washington, Jefferson, and Madison. Salomon also bribed a vast number of American politicians, going back to the US one-dollar bill. After the Declaration of Independence was drafted and ratified, Thomas Jefferson, Franklin, and John Adams were forced to meet, being obligated to pay back the cost of being entirely financed to defeat the British Empire in the American Revolutionary War. The price wasn't trivial. The Deep State wanted two things in return; to design the Great Seal, which was to be later printed on our currency, and permanent and full control over our Banking and Financial Institutions. Pierre Eugene Du Simitiere was called upon to join in the designing of The Great Seal, which was quickly approved. However, the Continental Congress would have nothing to do with it and did not approve it. The Rothschilds wanted their symbolism placed precisely as they asked to be in the Great

Seal of United States and would accept nothing less.

Nine years later, in 1782, Charles Thompson, Secretary of Congress, and William Barton assisted in facilitating an agreement on the design to be used in the Great Seal. Although some hostile opponents in the Continental Congress understood the symbolism in the design as illuminist, it was ultimately approved. "The Financier of the American Revolution" and yet another foreign agent

HISTORY OF THE DEEP STATE

made his mark in establishing an American Deep State.

The Deep State has injected a 'logic bomb' into our Republic or (The State) during and after we declared our Independence from the Crown of England. This is the only phrase in the English language that adequately explains how they have been planning to topple our Government and all Governments today. By the grace of God, we have President Trump, who is driving back the Deep State; However, rest assured these agencies, organizations, Corporations, Intelligence communities, Secret Societies, and Deep State-owned Media will, unfortunately still be here after Trump. Like a pervasive and insidious cancer, it is still in our nation's blood, infecting our culture, at a level, no one has ever seen. As long as our culture remains infected by the Quasi-Communist Ideology of The Deep State, we will eventually be overrun by this foreign power hierarchy; along with many other countries who also have their own shadow Government/Deep State.

Why would a hostile foreign State inject

various counties, especially the bacon of the free world with a 'Logic Bomb'? A logic bomb is defined as 'a set of parameters secretly incorporated into a program so that if a particular condition is satisfied, they will be carried out with destructive effects.' The United States is the program, so to speak, who's Deep States conditions are slowly being met are the breakdown of Westernized Government, Religious Institutions, the family,

and cultural norms. It is no coincidence that The Deep State does not only target each one of these institutions, but they have also nearly been completely usurped today. The

Deep State has embedded itself completely into the DOJ, and all U.S. intelligence communities. It has made its way into numbers religious Institutions, including but not exclusive to 'The Vatican,' essentially buying them out as one would a business, then spreading their own 'false doctrines.' The Rockefellers also targeted schools and institutions since the early 1920s. For many people the effects are very noticeable; however, the source remains mysterious. It's no mystery at all, once again here are the objectives as stated by Adam Weishaupt, the father of the Deep State:

I. Eradication of all Governments (Overthrowing the State)

II. Eradication of inheritance (Control over wealth and monetary distribution)

III. Eradication of property rights (Deep State Quasi-Communism)

IV. Eradication of Nationalism and Patriotism (Disbanding of Countries)

V. Population reduction (Rise of a New World Elitism)

VI. Eradication of religion (Satanism)

VII. Eradication of family (Secular Culture)

VIII. The formation of a New World Government (New World Order or a 'Deep State')

HISTORY OF THE DEEP STATE

These very objectives are virtually identical to the agenda of the left today, and although the elitists on the right feign opposition to these Communist Ideologies, their agenda is the same. When closely examining Presidential Candidates throughout our Nation's history, they very often would run as 'Centrists' or 'Moderates,' or in Obama's case, there was no message at all; then radically shift from the center to the left, subtly throughout their Presidency.

"Because liberalism typically doesn't sell in American presidential politics, liberal candidates tend to run as culturally conservative centrists."

- Rich Lowry

While liberal Presidential candidates traditionally run as centrists to curry favor from voters, Conservative Presidential Candidates do the same. The overuse of the word bipartisan and the phrase 'working across the aisle,' can be found in every Presidential campaign. 'Bipartisan' has always been the Deep States subliminal mantra used to curry favor among the brainwashed left, right and independent. It is a meaningless word since no voters are centrists, voters are usually just too confused to decide which Candidate is the lesser of two evils. Since both parties run as moderates or centrists, voting becomes a coin toss.

The public has been mind-controlled by The Deep State. The so-called Independent voter (incidentally statistics show that Independent voters are always the critical demographic who decides the outcome of an election) is only Independent because he has been programmed to be. What is the centrist's mantra? Usually, it is some variation of, 'I'm fiscally Conservative but

socially Liberal.' This defies all logic, because, these Independents are really saying that, they save money like a Conservative, but spend more like a Liberal. The Deep States programming is insidious and growing Nationally and Globally.

Mind control and mob hypnosis in Main Stream Media hasn't changed since ancient times. The Deep State Illuminists know how useful it is, only too well. Studies show that visual learning is fifty thousand times faster and more efficient than traditional teaching methods, but without the details. Emotionally charged graphics accomplish two things; cognitively we see everything we need to understand with no words. If the Images are emotionally charged, we especially become attached to those images, never forgetting them.

Are you thinking about 9/11 right now? Why it has not happened yet? All of the emotionally charged images you've been forced to be subjected to were published in the 70's and 80's, one in 1975, twenty-six years before 9/11! The Deep State Media are not psychics, but somehow thousands of similar images of dire warnings of impending doom, involving planes crashing into the Twin Towers have managed to bombard our minds with unforgettable images, forever burned into our psyche.

113 | HISTORY OF THE DEEP STATE

Thousands of instances like these being found in advertisements, television shows, cartoons, magazines and in major motion pictures could not have been just a coincidence! <u>Does the Deep control all major media outlets? Yes.</u>

The image on the right appears to depict a tower collapsing with smoke and fire at the base of it; and can be found at  the left corner of the Illuminati pyramid, also on the back of the double-sided Great Seal, found on the one-dollar bill. Haym Solomon's push for the Deep State imagery and symbolism was designed in 1782. Was a horrific attack against our Republic (The State) planned and calculated over 230 years in advance, by the same Deep State who blackmailed us into being controlled by their Foreign-owned Banks and financial institutions? The Deep States stated objective is a one world Government, abolishing all Governments, religions, and property. In line with the same principles found in the Order of the Illuminati, The New World Order's objectives are the same but have been expounded upon, only now it has an even more powerful set of teeth. 'Novus Ordo Seclorum' - New World Order.

CHAPTER FIVE
THE MILITARY INDUSTRIAL COMPLEX

"Military men are dumb, stupid animals to be used as pawns for foreign policy."

- Illuminatus, Henry Kissinger

↳ *also a Bilderberger scary —*

When President Eisenhower gave this Farewell Address given on January 17, 1961, now made famous for his reference to, what he called a 'Military Industrial Complex.' Pundits, Historians, and even philosophers have been arguing what Eisenhower meant by this. Even in the context of the rest of the lengthy speech, they have never come close to a definitive explanation. Because this was the first time anyone publicly used this phrase, it's deeper meaning is still confusing for the elite. Eisenhower was, very simply, sending a message to the incoming President, John F. Kennedy of a Globalized Deep State and Communist threat, which at that time involved a direct Nazi infiltration and corruption of all of our Intelligence Agencies. Perhaps he was too cowardly to confront them himself, but at the very least was brave enough to broadcast the message for the incoming Presidents, and for all future Presidents of The United States of America. This would explain why this now historical 'Military Industrial Complex Speech' was given only three days prior to him leaving Office.

Before that day, no mention of a grave threat from a 'Military Industrial Complex' was ever mentioned, but in giving this warning, he would prepare the way for President John F Kennedy. That is, of course assuming he would be able to ward off such a grave threat alone. This dire warning given was concerning the threat of more 'unwarranted' threats, to be given falsely in the name of 'National Security,' in an attempt to foment full-scale Nuclear War. 'The Military Industrial Complex' is the Deep State Military; meaning while there is a time for war, the MIC foments wars and 'false flag attacks' in an effort to funnel vast sums of money to corrupt Congressmen, politicians, and foreign investors. Trillions of dollars that have been allocated to the Defense budget and into defensive spending and are still unaccounted for today. While it is incredibly important to have a powerful Military, which today is not only second to none. The Military was strong then, but today it has become utterly undefeatable, and should only be used carefully, during a real posed threat; not a fomented Deep State crisis:

"My fellow Americans: Three days from now, after half a century in the service of our country, I shall lay down the responsibilities of office as, in traditional and solemn ceremony, the authority of the Presidency is vested in my successor.

Like every other citizen, *I wish the new President, and all who will labor with him, Godspeed. I pray that the coming years will be blessed with peace and prosperity for all*--our people expect their President and the Congress to find essential agreement on issues of great moment, the wise resolution of which will better shape the future of the Nation..*We now stand ten years past the midpoint of a century that has witnessed four major wars among great nations. Three of these involved our own country.* Despite these holocausts America is today the strongest, the most influential and most productive nation in the world. Understandably proud of this pre-eminence, we yet realize that **America's leadership and prestige depend, not merely upon our unmatched material progress, riches and military strength, but on how we use our power in the interests of world peace and human betterment...**

We face a hostile ideology — global in scope, atheistic in character, ruthless in purpose, and insidious in method.

HISTORY OF THE DEEP STATE

*Unhappily the danger it poses promises to be of indefinite duration... Only thus shall we remain, despite every provocation, on our charted course toward permanent peace and human betterment..*rises there will continue to be. In meeting them, whether foreign or domestic...A huge increase in newer elements of our defense; **development of unrealistic programs** to cure every ill in agriculture; a dramatic expansion in basic and applied research... ***But each proposal (Proposed Crises) must be weighed in the light of a broader consideration:*** the need to maintain balance in and among national programs — balance between the private and the public economy, balance between cost and hoped for advantage — balance between the clearly necessary and the comfortably desirable; balance between our essential requirements as a nation and the duties imposed by the nation upon the individual; **balance between actions of the moment and the national welfare of the future.**

Good judgment seeks balance and progress; lack of it eventually finds imbalance and frustration. Our military organization today bears little relation to that known by any of my predecessors in peacetime, or indeed by the fighting men of World War II or Korea.

Until the latest of our world conflicts, the United States had no armaments industry. American makers of plowshares could, with time and as required, make swords as well. But now we can no longer risk emergency improvisation of national defense; we have been compelled to create a permanent armaments industry of vast proportions. Added to this, three and a half million men and women are directly engaged in the defense establishment. **We annually spend on military security more than the net income of all United States corporations.** This conjunction of an immense military establishment and a large arms industry is new in the American experience. **The total influence — economic, political, even spiritual — is**

HISTORY OF THE DEEP STATE

felt in every city, every State house, every office of the Federal government. We recognize the imperative need for this development. Yet we must not fail to comprehend its grave implications. *Our toil, resources and livelihood are all involved; so is the very structure of our society.*

In the councils of government, we must guard against the acquisition of unwarranted influence, whether sought or unsought, by the military industrial complex. The potential for the disastrous rise of misplaced power exists and will persist...

Akin to, and **largely responsible for the sweeping changes in our industrial-military posture, has been the technological revolution during recent decades. Today, the solitary inventor, tinkering in his shop, has been overshadowed by task forces of scientists in laboratories and testing fields**

(Operation Paperclip). In the same fashion, the free university, historically the fountainhead of free ideas and scientific discovery, has experienced a revolution in the conduct of research. Partly because of the huge costs involved, ***a government contract becomes virtually a substitute for intellectual curiosity.*** For every old blackboard there are now hundreds of new electronic computers.

The prospect of domination of the nation's scholars by Federal employment, project allocations, and the power of money is ever present (Deep State Nazi Invasion) and is gravely to be regarded. Yet, in holding scientific research and discovery in respect, as we should, we must also be alert to the equal and opposite danger that ***public policy could itself become the captive of a scientific technological elite…***

Another factor in maintaining balance involves the element of time. As we peer into society's future, we — you and I, and our government — ***must avoid the impulse to live only for today, plundering, for our own ease and convenience, the precious resources of tomorrow.*** We cannot mortgage the material assets of our grandchildren without risking the loss also of their political and spiritual heritage. ***We want democracy to survive for all generations to come, not to become the insolvent phantom of tomorrow...***

Disarmament, with mutual honor and confidence, is a continuing imperative. Together we must learn how to compose differences, not with arms, but with intellect and decent purpose. Because this need is so sharp and apparent ***I confess that I lay down my official responsibilities in this field with a definite sense of disappointment.*** As one who has witnessed the horror and the lingering sadness of war — as one who knows that another war could utterly destroy this civilization which has been so slowly and painfully built over thousands of years — **I wish I could say tonight that a lasting peace is in sight."**

- January 17, 1961, Eisenhower's Farewell Address

The one thing and only thing that pundits can agree on about Eisenhower's 'Military Industrial Complex' Speech, is that its theme was undeniably centered around pervasive Communism, but that is the general theme. A closer look at this speech reveals a deeper understanding of a Communist infiltration from inside our very own Government:

1) "Today, the solitary inventor, tinkering in his shop, has been overshadowed by task forces of scientists in laboratories and testing fields."

2) "The prospect of domination of the nation's scholars by Federal employment, project allocations, and the power of money is ever present and is gravely to be regarded."

3) "We must also be alert to the equal and opposite danger that public policy could itself become the captive of a scientific-technological elite."

These were Eisenhower's words, and were very directly speaking to a private Government operation known as 'Operation Paperclip.' Between 1945 and 1959 an estimated 3,000 Nazis were secretly smuggled into the United States which was approved by Illuminatus, President Harry Truman.

Operation Paperclip began with fifteen hundred high ranking Nazis, who were captured during 'The Nuremberg Trials' and were supposed to stand trial to be prosecuted, tried, convicted, then hung for 'Crimes against Humanity.' Of course, these 1,500 top Nazis never stood trial, but instead were secretly smuggled into The United States into various cities throughout Florida and Boston, MA, via The Deep State's use of Special Agents in Army CIC. These three thousand Nazis were then thoroughly embedded into the CIA, FBI, DOJ, and NASA, under Operation Paperclip. This was the third wave of the Deep States evolution, making the Deep State even more powerful than ever before; now having full control over and weaponizing all of our Governments Intelligence Agencies.

Among the three thousand Nazis who were smuggled into the United States, was George Herbert Walker Bush's father, Prescott Bush during Operation Paperclip. His son would then later become Director of the C.I.A. the 41st U.S President of the United States, and founder of the New World Order in 1981.

Prescott Bush was not the only Nazi embedded into The Deep State, many of them were top Nazi scientists, physicists, and engineers; bringing with them a vast Deep State upgrade, from even the thousands of Communists who were also embedded into the CIA, FBI, DOJ and State Department by The Rockefellers in the 1920's (The second wave of Deep State). While a fraction of these three thousand Nazis were placed into the CIA's MK Ultra Mind Control Program and the research into the effects of L.S.D.; the top

Nazis who were smuggled in, like Wernher Von Braun who became the first director of Marshall Space Flight Center.

Not only were military defense and Intelligence agencies undermined, but a man named Kurt Debus, who worked with Von Braun during the Nazis V-2 rocket testing's, also became Director of The Kennedy Space Center. Arthur Rudolph also worked for the Nazis to build advanced Nazi rocketry and was smuggled into the U.S.'s Deep State to become Director of the NASA Saturn 500 program.

Before going any further, it is also important to note, that while Illuminatus's financers, Communists, and Nazis were sent to infiltrate our Country; they have consistently changed their names to avoid public scrutiny. The Rothchild's are the best example of this, as may not even be of Jewish descent at all, but have, without question adopted this phony name. (The Rothchild's do not practice Judaism, in fact, they fomented the rise of Hitler, Nazi Germany, and World War II) entirely (this will be explained in detail in a later chapter).

Walter Durenberger who was also among the 3,000 Deep State Agents smuggled in from Nazi Germany became one of the leading engineers in the development of Deep State Nazi rocketry, and before a National Space industry conference said:

"Gentleman. I didn't come to this country to lose a third World War, I already lost the first two!"

–Walter Durenberger

Major General Walton Durenberger was recruited directly by Hitler himself to work for Nazis, also became Vice President of Bell Aerospace Corporation. In the above statement, it is clear, with no unwavering semantics, that Durenberger wasn't preparing for World War 3; He was planning it! Durenberger was fighting on the wrong side of World War 1 and WW2, considering both to be utter losses. The Deep State has been planning the fomentation of World War III since the 50's when the Nazis were brought over here. In keeping with the Order of the Illuminati, The Nazis primary objective is also the toppling of all Governments (by utilizing the catastrophic effects of Globalization and Communism) and the formation of a one World Government, A.K.A. The New World Order. (Visions for 2020, published by NASA, much of which was written and co-written by the same Nazi's who were smuggled into the U.S., states that there will be 'a widening gap between the haves and have-nots' due to Globalization.) This chilling statement portends of a Globalized World of the future, whereas instability arises around the World, an opening for another World War Three is precisely what they are waiting for.

It's also important to keep in mind that NASA functions as a 'Civilian Space Military,' controlling all airspace; and since NASA runs completely Independent from the United

States Military its motives become even more questionable given it is believed that NASA may also have access nuclear weapons.

The Gulf War, where Bush Sr. talked about the importance of a 'New World Order' Ad Nauseum, ironically is where the Deep State began the first testing of our New World Order weaponry. The B2 Stealth Bomber was first used and proved our military to be unrivaled by any country of the World. The UAV or Unmanned Aerial Vehicle nicknamed 'The Predator' was also first used during the Gulf War, now commonly referred to as 'Drones,' was also utilized by Obama in Afghanistan.

Obama's Deep State Administration intentionally weakened our military position throughout the world, so that an incoming President may, in fact, be forced to use a now unrivaled Military Industrial Complex, during or after some preemptive attack.

HISTORY OF THE DEEP STATE

The New World Order, which was brought to us by the Nazis, did, in fact, develop our Military Industrial Complex to a new level, far surpassing any Country in the world. We are virtually an unbeatable Military at this point in time. When so-called Military pundits say it, they don't understand the degree to which this statement is true. We are continually being told of the developing threat of China etc. when the truth is no countries have the Air Superiority that we do, and the Media very often downplays our Military superiority. Nuclear weapons in China are vastly outnumbered by our own. That being said, without a significant threat posed in sight, how can a new war be fomented? The Deep State will continue to look for ways to argue the need for wars around the world, where none exists.

In understanding The Deep States relentless use of 'false flags,' coupled with our unrivaled Military Industrial Complex, it is clear that The Deep State was anticipating Hillary Clinton to be our current President. Being a known war hawk, it is very likely that we could've been involved in an all-out World War, which is the objective of the New World Order. It is the first phase in utilizing a Military Industrial Complex, using a series of false Flags to promote Wars in various countries like North Korea, China, Russia, Etc.

In the hands of a sensible leader, like President Trump, who is willing to negotiate peace talks before calling for all-out war, The Military Industrial Complex now becomes a defensive mechanism for peace. As for what is to come after President Trump, there are no guarantees. Somehow, like John F. Kennedy, President Trump will have to try to find a way to eliminate The Deep State. Although Kennedy was unsuccessful, he did boldly attempt to do it, in the interest of what was best for this Country. Until its hostile and foreign influence is wholly driven out of our country, we will continue to be faced with the Deep States primary goal, which is overthrowing The United States ('The State').

HISTORY OF THE DEEP STATE

As Eisenhower so correctly phrased in his warning," In the councils of government, we must guard against the acquisition of unwarranted influence, whether sought or unsought, by the Military Industrial Complex."

1776 – 1783: American Revolutionary War

1784 – 1795: Northwest Indian War

1811: Tecumseh's War

1812 – 1815: War of 1812

1816 – 1824: Piracy war

1827: Winnebago War

1831: Sac and Fox Indian War

1832: Black Hawk War

1837 -1839: Cherokee Indian War

1840: U.S. Military occupation of the Fiji Islands

1846 – 1848: Mexican-American War

1861 -1865: American Civil War

1849 – 1896: U.S. Military occupation of Mexico

1898: Spanish-American War

1899 – 1913: Philippine-American War

1914 – 1918: World War I

1920 – 1934: Banana Wars

1939 -1945: World War II

1946: Occupation of the Philippines and South Korea

1950 – 1953: Korean War

1955 – 1962: U.S. Military policing of Vietnam.

1963 – 1975: Vietnam War

1979 – 1986: Cold War

1987 – 1989: Persian Gulf Conflict

1990 – 1991: Gulf War

1992 – 1996: Conflict in Iraq

HISTORY OF THE DEEP STATE

1998: Destabilization of Iraq

1999: Kosovo War

2001 – 2011: War on Terrorism in Afghanistan and Iraq

CHAPTER SIX
THE BAVARIAN BLOODLINE

"I know thy works, and tribulation, and poverty, but thou art rich and I know the blasphemy of them which say they are Jews, and are not, but are the synagogue of Satan."

- Revelation 2:9

To better understand The Deep State, and their history – we must understand that their roots are not Judean at all, the Bavarian bloodline from which they descend is a pure Pagan bloodline, with absolutely no relationship to Jews. Remember the second precept of 'The order of the Illuminati':

I) Masonic secrets – Good and Evil
II) Sufism – Islamic practices
III) Hatha Yoga – Practices in mental discipline

Without going much further into the meaning of this, as most people are aware, Islam and Judaism are, for the most part, in complete opposition to each other. The Illuminati's practice of Islamic teachings directly opposes its façade of being seemingly Jewish. So why would anyone want to claim to be Jews, while not in fact being Jewish? In case it hasn't been made crystal clear by now, we are dealing with masters of deception and confusion. Furthermore, to better understand the infiltration of the Jewish and Christian faiths by these illuminists, let's recall one of their major Objectives; Abolition of Religion. One cannot be a Muslim, a Jew, a Satanist, and an Atheist all at the same time. Just as one cannot serve Christ and Satan. The Deep State understands this all too well; to undermine a Government, you must first undermine its Religious Institutions, Family, and Culture. The Deep State operates by toppling Governments from the inside, out. Why is this so important and how does it relate to The Bavarian bloodlines?

First, let's begin with the now German State of Bavaria. If you've ever been there or looked at photographs of Bavaria, or what is now the Bavarian State of Germany, you will see it is a magnificent place. Some of the most beautiful landscapes, mountains, countryside, castles, and architecture can be found here. If it seems too good to be true,

HISTORY OF THE DEEP STATE

that's because it is. How could such a magnificent place be so backward and Satanic? You might say, 'I've been to Bavaria, and I have never seen anyone Satanic!' Then you simply don't understand its history. Not only do the vast majority of the Deep State elect (Presidents, Monarchy, and Kings) originate from Bavaria, its seemingly harmless culture has now overtaken nearly every Nation in the world. All of the 13 Illuminati bloodlines didn't begin in 1776 with a top illuminist randomly drawing names out of a hat; instead, they originated from one single family, and over time became 13 Bavarian families, with related families and Dynasties. All told, there may be roughly

169 Bavarian Deep State families dispersed and embedded into politics:

THE ASTOR BLOODLINE

THE BUNDY BLOODLINE

THE COLLINS BLOODLINE

THE DUPONT BLOODLINE

THE FREEMAN BLOODLINE

THE KENNEDY BLOODLINE

THE LI BLOODLINE

THE ONASSIS BLOODLINE

THE REYNOLDS BLOODLINE

THE ROCKEFELLER BLOODLINE

THE ROTHSCHILD BLOODLINE

THE RUSSELL BLOODLINE

THE VAN DUYN BLOODLINE

All of these 169 families could easily fill an encyclopedia to explain in detail. There are 13 Illuminati Dynasties, and out of each one of these Dynasties are another 13 families giving us a total of 169 Bavarian families who infiltrate and subjugate our world.

But, why are there any such families at all, who would want to do such horrific things? Once we go back into the history of Bavaria, it will become clear exactly how this became possible.

"During the First World War, I told her, Hitler had been a runner, delivering messages between the German trenches, and he was disgusted by seeing his fellow soldiers visit French brothels. To keep the Aryan bloodlines pure, and prevent the spread of venereal disease, he commissioned an inflatable doll that Nazi troops could take into battle. Hitler himself designed the dolls to have blond hair and large breasts. The Allied firebombing of Dresden destroyed the factory before the dolls could ever go into wide distribution."

- Chuck Palahniuk

I would like to first preface this history, with a look into the theological background of the origins of bloodlines. The Free Masons have been studying good and evil with the hope of becoming wise and illuminated. For its members that are at the middle and bottom of the hierarchy, it is not likely to ever happen.

The Illuminati had Adam Weishaupt (A Bavarian) take Free Masonry to an extremist level in its application, he, however, did have a complete understanding of the Bible, as it applies to traditional Christianity and

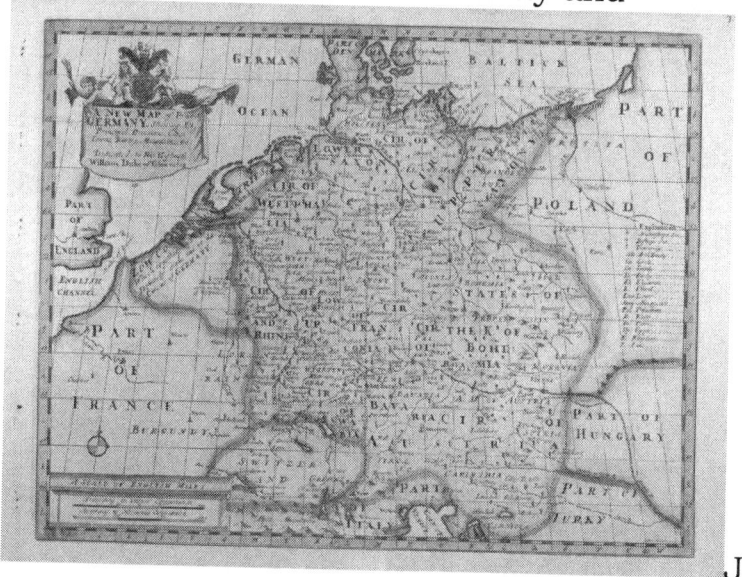

Judaism; with a complete understanding of both, and being immersed in it daily for

decades. Only someone like this could unravel evil in its purest sense. Although his vast understanding of Judaism and Christianity (Jesuit Catholicism) was used for evil, it also explains where and how precisely he reversed engineered God so perfectly. In his quest for the antithesis to God, Gods law, and Gods people, he organized his own bloodline, narrowing it down to the evillest among the already Pagan Bavarian bloodline. After overthrowing Nations, only members of these thirteen bloodlines would be allowed to become rulers of those Nations.

145 | HISTORY OF THE DEEP STATE

As a former practicing Jew and Catholic, Weishaupt understood that the Torah was also an archive of the Jewish Kings and family bloodlines. It was also the end of the religious application of a bloodline altogether, as Christianity emerged, it made the Jewish bloodline obsolete. For Christians, there is no bloodline. Jesus would be the end of the Jewish bloodline since he opened the practice of Christianity to every race. This marked the end of a Jewish bloodline, with the ushering in of Christianity (no bloodlines); and would leave an opening for Weishaupt to extend a contrived and phony Jewish bloodline, not ordained by God. Though the bloodline would appear to be real, the effect of extending a phony Jewish bloodline would no doubt draw an endless stream of newly indoctrinated and deceived recruits. This bloodline also achieved his goal to permanently perverting Judaism as a religion, while also subverting Christianity; as the Torah is the Old Testament of the Christian Bible. The goal here was to trick people into believing that these Kings, Presidents, Prime ministers and Royalty are related to Jewish Kings and Jesus Christ. The beginnings of his subversion of prominent Religious Institutions were now in place.

147 | HISTORY OF THE DEEP STATE

If it were not for this solitary sick man, we would not have a Deep State or a New World Order that we can now see throughout our world and embedded into our Government today. Still, the Bavarian culture was doing what all cultures do; cultivating an ideology that would eventually bring forth a man who would fully understand it, then extort it for all manner of evil. The culture is more to blame than the man behind it. The Bavarians were mystics, occultists, witches, sorcerers, and most importantly, a full-blown Pagan culture. Even eight hundred years after Christ, the Bavarians were essentially backwoods Pagans, and when exposed to modern day Christianity rejected it outright, continuing onward, practicing the traditions of their Pagan forefathers.

The Free Masons and eventually Illuminists both fervently studied other religious teachings, though mostly focusing their attention on the Bible and the Torah. Remember, their goal was not to understand God, so much as it was to understand what they perceived as wisdom; and most of all, a complete understanding of Satan; by way of a complete understanding of God. While this is not taught inside their temples, Weishaupt connected the dots very quickly as to the true meaning behind Free Masonry and did not see the need to waste any more time further, getting directly to the heart of their doctrine.

When pronouncing his understanding of the secrets behind Free Masonry, his doctrine quickly spread like wildfire throughout Europe, and within just a matter of months, Secret Societies were being set up within Free Mason Secret Societies. As each year, decade, and century passed, the fire deepened until a man, also a Bavarian began to hear his message; but did not take it lightly; instead pushed Weishaupt's ideas even further by putting his stated objectives into action. Hitler was immediately noticed by the Rothchild's, (also living in Bavaria) and saw the rise of Hitler as an incredible 'Military Industrial Complex' investment. The Rothchild's completely funded Hitler's rise to power.

A nobody named Adolf Hitler living in Bavaria, who fought in World War 1, diseased and blinded for a time, completely destitute and poor, came out of obscurity to become the next man rule the world? The world does not work that way, and the real story behind Hitler and his rise to power and the fomentation of World War II, can be found with his work with President Harry Truman, via the CIA, and being entirely financed and backed by the Rothchild's.

It is worth pointing out that Hitler's occultists' beliefs were in complete accord with those of the Order of the Illuminati; perhaps with the exception that the Illuminati do not seem to be race-exclusive. Hitler believed in The Order of the Illuminati's principles and eventually put all of their objectives of the abolition of Governments, family, religion, and practicing of Islamic teachings into action. Not to mention their kinship in their hate for the true Jewish people, and their goal of a One World Government. President Franklin D. Roosevelt and President Truman were both also involved with the fomentation of World War II, working alongside Joe Kennedy, the Unofficial Ambassador between The Nazis, Great Britain, and The United States. Joe Kennedy and the Rothchild's were fomenting the War as an excuse to line corrupt politician's pockets with wartime monies (MIC). Ending World War II, Harry Truman made himself a hero, saving the world from the World War he, himself allowed to happen.

151 | HISTORY OF THE DEEP STATE

Although Hitler was not born in Bavaria, he moved and settled into Munich, Germany in 1913. Munich, of course, is the Capital of Bavaria and is its most densely populated city. Everything you could ever hope to learn about its long Pagan history and culture is in Munich, waiting to be discovered as a way of life. As you can see from this map of Germany, which is one of Germanys first maps, outlining all of its modern regions and borders. You can see, if you'll take notice, that the 'State of Bohemia' was also a part of what is now the Bavarian State of Germany; and as many of you may already be aware, the now famous 'Bohemian Society' indeed took its name from what it considers to be this very 'Sacred' part of Germany.

The Bohemians and the Bavarians are the same culture, people, and share the same ancient history, rich with of same Bavarian family bloodlines. Again, as has been established: Weishaupt's Illuminati, the Rothchild's, Hitler, Nazi Germany, and The Bavarian Society have all come out of this single and very specific region of Germany known as Bavaria.

Where did the Kings and elite political class of the Roman Empire flee to after the collapse of their World Empire? The Deep State Roman Empire went to Bavaria and Bohemia, now simply the German State of Bavaria. The five centuries long World-Dominated Roman Empire began in 31 B.C. and ended in 476 A.D. With 507 years' worth of amassed worldwide plunder under its belt, Its Empire and Military fell, but its culture and great wealth did not. The first King of The Roman Empire was Gaius Octavian Thurinus, but the origins of Roman Empire go back even further; to the beginning of Rome, 753 B.C., with King Romulus.

The Etruscans pre-dated the Romans, King Romulus, and Roman Empire, who had the same Culture, Gods, and writings of both the Greeks and Romans; both sharing the traditions of the Etruscans, who predated both the Greeks and Romans. This suggests that the Roman Empires Elite were an amalgamated race of the Greeks, Etruscans,

HISTORY OF THE DEEP STATE

Albanians, Italians, Cyprians, Turkish, and Egyptians. The elites of the Roman empire were not pure Italian, and this can be evidenced in examining their statues, art, and sculptures. The most important connection between all of these peoples was their practice of worshiping the Saturn God.

The offerings and Sacrifices can be found in every appearance of all of the aforenamed cultures; with the Etruscan God, Satres, The Greek God, Cronus (who was deified for devouring children), the Carthaginian God

Ba'al Hammon, (also involving child sacrifice), The Greek God, 'EL'

was also another name for their Saturn God (incidentally, the word elite derives from: the Greek 'El', meaning Saturn God, and the Greek suffix 'ite', denoting tribes and doctrines; the Elite, or the tribe of Saturn worship). All Bavarian and Illuminati Bloodlines originate from the bloodline of the Ancient Greeks; more specifically, the Godfather of the Pagan Deep State, Alexander the Great.

CHAPTER SEVEN

THE CFR, THE U.N & THE WORLD COURT

"A single world economic system is essential for the final triumph of Socialism."

- Lenin

If there is a deadlock or a dispute on the Deep States decisions made at the United Nations, the World Court supersedes and takes precedence over any United Nations decisions. The Council on Foreign Relations is a Communist and Deep State agency, controlling Domestic and World affairs. The CFR not only controls the United Nations, but it also is controls the State Department, CIA, FBI, NATO, Department of Justice, Anti-American Political Activism, the toppling of

Governments through Communistic means, the false fomentation of Wars and World Wars, and virtually every Media outlet in America and around the world.

The Council on Foreign Relations has 1,800 members. These members are comprised of the top hierarchy of elitist global industries, education propagandists, and the Deep State Agenda-driven Main Stream Media. It is not clear whether every one of its members are intimately aware of their agenda. However, the agenda they have launched has been made quite clear over the last century as exhibiting a pattern of being Communist-driven.

Deep State and foreign Governments nominate members of both The CFR and World Court judges. The World Court is made up of 13 Judges from the Nations of their choosing. Seven from these thirteen make up the World Courts quorum, which only 4 of these seven is needed to make a final decision. Of the many foundations who have been active contributors to the CFR's World Court are The Rockefeller Foundation, and it

HISTORY OF THE DEEP STATE

is estimated that between 1925 and 1952, the Rockefeller Foundation donated over 11 million dollars to just the education component of the CFR, The American Council of Learned Societies alone; working with Harry Truman, in an effort to undermine American Acedia and the Public-School System with a hard-leftist agenda. Today we can clearly see that they have succeeded in satisfying meeting their goals.

The CFR's use of untraceable foundations is too numerous to mention, and the collection of wealth is still dispersed and funneled from the same prominent foreign Banking Institutions that have been investing in our Deep State Banks and Federal Reserve. The members of The Word Court and CFR are not taxed and run completely independent from any Government agency.

There are many components to the CFR, World Court and United Nations, two of which is the Bilderberg Group and the Trilateral Commission, both owned, in part by the Rockefellers.

Listed below are statements which I believe speak for themselves given from 'The Reece Committee Report', 'The Smoot Report', Prominent Politicians, and credible Reporters on the policies and the Globalized Communist influence disseminated from the C.F.R., The World Court, The United Nations, NATO, its other compartmentalized components, and referencing the CFR controlled Main Stream Media:

"Today the path to total dictatorship in the United States can be laid by strictly legal means, unseen and unheard by the Congress, the President, or the people, outwardly we have a Constitutional government; We have operating within our government and political system, another body representing another form of government, a bureaucratic elite which believes our Constitution is outmoded (The Deep State) and is sure that it is the winning side. All the strange developments in foreign policy agreements may be traced to this group who are going to make us over to suit their pleasure. We must consider our danger not

only in the terms of the treaties or agreements which have been completed, but in terms of those still in the pipelines, or already in effect, but still invisible to Congress or to the people. This political action group has its own local political support organizations, its own pressure groups, its own vested interests, its foothold within our government, and its own propaganda apparatus. Someone, somewhere, conceived the brilliant strategy of revolution by the assembly line. The pattern for total revolution was divided into separate parts, each of them as innocent, safe, and familiar-looking as possible. The men who made the blueprints know exactly what the final product is to be. They have planned the final assembly years ahead."

- *Senator William Jenner, 1954*

"What is the Establishment's viewpoint? Through the Roosevelt, Truman, Eisenhower, and Kennedy Administrations, its ideology is constant: that the best way to fight Communism is by a One World, Socialist State

governed by 'experts' like themselves. The result has been policies which favor the growth of the super-state, gradual surrender of U.S. sovereignty to the United Nations, and a steady retreat in the face of Communist aggression."

- Columnist, Edith Kermit

"The Council on Foreign Relations is the invisible government of the United States by virtue of the fact that members of the Council occupy key posts in the Executive branch of Government from the Presidency downward. By its own efforts, and through many interlocking organizations, the Council on Foreign Relations also virtually controls public opinion in the United States."

- The Smoot Report, July 17, 1961

"Make more effective use of the International Court of Justice, jurisdiction of which should be increased by withdrawal of reservations by member nations on matters judged to be domestic."

- Council on Foreign Relations Study No. 7 on 'The U.S. The World Court."

"Nationalism seldom yields positive doctrine, beyond the demand for a sovereign state, independent of alien overlords. While based on mass support, it is not necessarily democratic. Nationalism does, however, have much to contribute to the development of new countries, by providing a sense of social and political solidarity; and injecting dynamism and political activism into the society."

- Council on Foreign Relations, Study No. 10

"Substantial evidence indicates there is more than a mere close working-together among some foundations operating in the international field. There is here a close interlock. The Carnegie Endowment for International Peace, the Rockefeller

Foundation, and recently the Ford Foundation, joined by some others, have commonly cross-financed to the tune of many millions various intermediate and agency organizations concerned with internationalism, among them The Institute of Pacific Relations, The Foreign Policy Association, The Council on Foreign Relations and others."

-The Reece Committee Report

"The challenge of the future is to make this world one world -a world truly free to engage in common and constructive intellectual efforts that will serve the welfare of mankind everywhere. However well-meaning the advocates of complete Internationalism may be, they often play into the hands of the Communists. Communists recognize that a breakdown of Nationalism is a prerequisite to the introduction of Communism."

- The Rockefeller Foundation's statement during The Reece Committee Hearings, 1946

"In speed of transportation and communication, and in economic interdependence, the nations of the globe are already one world; the task is to secure recognition and acceptance of this oneness in the thinking of the people, so that the concept of one world may be realized psychologically, socially, and, in good time, politically. It is this task in particular that challenges the scholars and teachers to lead the way toward a new way of thinking. There is an urgent need for a program for world citizenship that can be made a part of every person's general education."

- The President's Commission on Higher Education

"It is a conclusion of this committee that the trustees of some of the major foundations have, on numerous important occasions, been beguiled by truly subversive influences. Without many of their trustees having the remotest idea of what has happened, these foundations have frequently been put substantially to uses which have adversely affected the best interests of the United States. The Cox Committee record shows that a conscious plan by the Communists was inaugurated to infiltrate the foundations for the purpose of appropriating their funds to Communist uses. We know from the evidence that the Communists succeeded in the case of seven foundations: The Marshall Field Foundation; the Garland Fund; the John Simon Guggenheim Foundation; the Heckscher Foundation; the Robert Marshall Foundation; the Rosenwald Fund; and the Phelps-Stokes Fund; and we are aware of the tragic result to our nation and to the world of Communist infiltration into the Institute of Pacific Relations. We also know that Communists and their fellow travelers had been able to secure grants from other foundations, including Carnegie and Rockefeller. We know, further, what the Cox Committee referred to as the ugly unalterable fact that Alger Hiss became the President."

- The Reece Committee Report

HISTORY OF THE DEEP STATE

"The Council on Foreign Relations came to be in essence an agency of the United States Government, no doubt carrying its internationalist bias with it. When World War II broke out, it offered its assistance to the Secretary of State. As a result, under the Council's Committee on Studies, the Rockefeller Foundation initiated and financed certain studies on: Security and Armaments Problems; Economic and Financial Problems; Political Problems; and Territorial Problems. These were actually known as the War and Peace Studies. Later this project was actually taken over by the State Department itself, engaging the secretaries who had been serving with the Council on Foreign Relations groups. A fifth subject was added in 1942 through the "Peace Aims Group." There was a precedent for this. The Carnegie Endowment had offered its services to the Government in both World War I and World War II. There was even an interlock in personnel in the person of Professor James T. Shotwell and many others, some of whom proceeded into executive and consultative office in the Government. There can be no doubt that much of the thinking in the State Department came from the personnel of the Carnegie Endowment and the Council on Foreign Relations. What we see here is a number of large foundations, primarily The Rockefeller Foundation, The Carnegie Corporation of New York, and the Carnegie Endowment for International Peace, using their enormous public funds to finance a one-sided approach to foreign policy and to promote it actively, among the public by propaganda, and in the Government through infiltration."

- The Reece Committee Report

"The Council (on Foreign Relations) did not amount to a great deal until 1927 when the Rockefeller family began to pour money into it. Before long, the Carnegie Foundation began to finance the Council. In 1929 the Council acquired its present headquarters property, the Harold Pratt House, 58 E. 86th St., New York City. In 1939 the Council began to take over the American State Department."

- The Smoot Report, June 12, 1961

The Report of the Council on Foreign Relations lists its members in 1960 and 1962, which include prominent members of the Main Stream Media:

Joseph C. Harsch, European Correspondent, Marquis Childs, syndicated columnist, Simon and Schuster, Inc., Gardner Cowles, of Cowles Magazine Co ., Publisher and President, Washington Times & Times Herald, publishers National Broadcasting Company (NBC), Palmer Hoyt, Publisher, Denver Post, Sam A. Jaffe, Joseph Barnes, Editor, Chairman of the Board, Newsweek, CBS News, Walter Lippmann, Allen Grover, Vice President, Time, Inc. syndicated columnist, Henry R. Luce, Chairman, Executive Committee, Newsweek, Editor-in-Chief of Time Magazine, Life Magazine, Malcolm Muir, William S. Paley, Chairman and Director, Chairman of the Board and

Editor-in-Chief, McGraw-Hill Publishing Co., Columbia Broadcasting System (CBS), James Reston, public opinion pollster, President and Publisher, New Herald Tribune, Elmo Roper, NBC and Radio Corporation of America, Arthur Hays Sulzberger, Publisher and Chairman of the Board, New York Times, David Sarnoff, Director, editorial writer, New York Times, John Hay Whitney, William L. Shirer, author and news commentator.

"The Goal Is Government of All the World": But the Atlantic Pact, NATO, It can be one of the most positive moves in the direction of One World; and it becomes clear that the first step toward World Government cannot be completed until we have advanced on four fronts: the economic, the military, the political, and the social.

- Elmo Roper, The Council on Foreign Relations

"We now have political, economic, welfare, and propaganda organs in NATO above our

169 | HISTORY OF THE DEEP STATE

government and our Constitution. The NATO super-government is very interested in labor, especially the movement of immigrants from country to country. It has recommended that governments facilitate labor mobility between their countries. The One Worlders believe nations have no right to decide who may be admitted and denied admittance to their country. NATO is interested in uniform Social Security for member countries. Politically, NATO is the means by which the One World Super State is being assembled from above through the UN, and horizontally in NATO, SEATO, and the Organization of American States."

- Senator William E. Jenner, February 1956

"The central feature of NATO is the mushrooming of central institutions in response to newly felt common needs. The North Atlantic Council has remained the central policy organ, having jurisdiction over the political, economic, and military aspects of the alliance. Under it, however, an initially

unplanned civilian central structure has arisen, with coordinating functions far exceeding those of any other regional or universal international organization. A Council of Permanent Representatives of the member governments is in continuous session to work out details of joint policy or submit suggestions to the Council. It is assisted by a series of technical committees, staffed in part by governmental delegates and in part by members of the NATO Secretariat, who take directions from no single Government. Policy emerges as a result of discussion among governmental delegates and independent experts and ceases, therefore, to be exclusively an intergovernmental compromise."

- *Ernest B. Haas*

"We cannot even find out what is going on. A five-year report on NATO was compiled in November 1954. When, a few days ago, I asked for later information, I was told it was classified. That means, for executive agencies

only. NATO government agencies recommend policies on taxes, inflation, arms production and economics. What their recommendations are, we in Congress do not know; they are classified."

- *Senator William E. Jenner*

"Most of all, we welcome the Atlantic Convention's recommendation that the NATO Governments promptly establish a Special Governmental Commission to draw up plans within two years for the creation of a true Atlantic Community, suitably organized to meet the political, military and economic challenges of this era. This could permit the Commission to draft a Federal Constitution for an Atlantic Union."

- *Clarence Streit, February 1962*

"If the United Nations is an instrument of United States policy, it is only one of many instruments available to us. It is therefore important to be clear not only about what the

United Nations does but what it does not do clarity on this score helps solve the contradictions some people seem to find on American foreign policy, a contradiction between our reliance on the institutions of the Atlantic Community and our participation in the United Nations. No such contradiction, in fact, exists. The founders of the United Nations recognized the need for regional institutions and explicitly provided for them in the Charter; In practice, we use the various institutions to which we belong for quite different purposes. The North Atlantic Treaty Organization is the backbone of our military defense through the OECD, the Organization for Economic Cooperation and Development, we are developing means for close cooperation in economic matters with the larger industrialized powers on either side of the Atlantic."

- Secretary of State George Ball, 1962

"Although the Atlantic Community is steadily strengthening, even this is, in itself, not

enough. The interests of the Atlantic nations are global. Their vision demands a more universal goal, a world order in which all free nations can concert to achieve their common purposes, a community of free nations. Our broader and ultimate objective in all these efforts is a universal community of nations."

- Harlan Cleveland, January 31, 1962, Assistant Secretary of State and CFR member

in 1936 the Communist International formally presented its three-stage plan for achieving World Government, *Stage 1: Socialize the economies of all nations, particularly the Western capitalistic democracies, most particularly the United States;* Stage 2: *"Bring about federal unions of various groupings of the socialized nations, Stage 3: Amalgamate all of the federal unions into one world-wide union of Socialist states."*

- The Smoot Report, 1962

CHAPTER EIGHT
THE NEW WORLD ORDER

"This is an historic moment. We have in this past year made great progress in ending the long era of conflict and cold war. We have before us the opportunity to forge for ourselves and for future generations a new world order -- a world where the rule of law, not the law of the jungle, governs the conduct of nations. When we are successful - and we will be - we have a real chance at this New World Order, an order in which a credible United Nations can use its peacekeeping role to fulfill the promise and vision of the U.N.'s founders."

- George Herbert Walker Bush, 1991

Although the formation for the reality of a coming New World Order in the United States was brewing in 1981, it wasn't until 1991, during 'The Gulf War' with assistance the 'United Nations' where an unprecedented 39 countries were fighting alongside our own military; forming what was the Deep State's display of the first One-World Military. Our newly demonstrated Military dominance was advanced and unquestionably superior in its technology - especially as it relates to the Stealth B-2 Bomber, laser guided missiles, our ability to dominate all the world's airspace; and the first use of the UAV, being completely unseen and unmanned, and having the capability of striking any target with precision accuracy. This was The New World Order being applied in its 'testing phase'.

There is no question that this test phase (phase 1) of 'The New World Order' was very real, and with what seemed to be pure and good intentions on the surface for our Country's Dominance Militarily. There are, however, three grave concerns with this 'New World Orders' Gulf War 'test phase.' As beautiful as it was to have an unrivaled Military; it was the veiled first phase of the Deep States One World Military, being harmless at the surface, but with a sinister end game.

Indeed, George Herbert Walker Bush, the son of a Nazi, did demonstrate the incredible power of our new air superiority, which was clearly, second to none. This by itself, would've been an incredible achievement.

The first, second and third waves of The New World Order happened as detailed below:

FIRST NWO WAVE – Operation Desert Storm January 17th, 1991

SECOND NWO WAVE - September 11th, 2001

THIRD NWO WAVE: March 20th – May 1st, 2003, during the Invasion and destabilization of Iraq and the region.

HISTORY OF THE DEEP STATE

FORTH NWO WAVE – The Entirety of Obamas Presidency, pronounced in greater detail on January 25, 2011, during his State of the Union Address. A tool for the Deep State, Obama brought change. He radically indoctrinated the culture of the country as no Deep State President has ever done before.

The first reference of the phrase 'The New World Order' is believed by some, to come from the title of the book written at the beginning of World War II, by the Socialist-American writer, H.G. Wells. The Deep State Nazi sympathizer wrote:

"The New Deal is plainly an attempt to achieve a working socialism and avert a social collapse in America; it is extraordinarily parallel to the successive 'policies' and 'Plans' of the Russian experiment. Americans shirk the word 'socialism,' but what else can one call it?"

—H.G. Wells, *The New World Order*, 1939

However, H.G. Wells was not the first to coin the phrase 'The New World Order,' Adolf Hitler was! It was the title of his book, written from prison, aptly entitled, 'My New Order'! When interpreting the German phrase 'My New Order,' especially in the context of his book, is more precisely interpreted to mean 'THE NEW WORLD ORDER.' Hitler was indeed the father and founder of the New World Order! This is no small detail as it relates to the History of the world, America, and The Deep State; and seems to have been purposely suppressed by Deep State Historians:

"My feelings as a Christian point me to my Lord and Savior as a fighter. It points me to the man who once in loneliness, surrounded by a few followers, recognized these Jews for what they were and summoned men to fight against them and who, God's truth! Was greatest not as a sufferer but as a fighter. In boundless love as a Christian and as a man I read through the passage which tells us how the Lord, at last, rose in His might and seized the scourge to drive out of the Temple the

HISTORY OF THE DEEP STATE

brood of vipers and adders. How terrific was his fight against the Jewish poison? Today, after two thousand years, with deepest emotion I recognize more profoundly than ever before the fact that it was for this that He had to shed his blood upon the Cross. As a Christian, I have no duty to allow myself to be cheated, but I have the duty to be a fighter for truth and justice... And if there is anything which could demonstrate that we are acting rightly, it is the distress that daily grows. For as a Christian I have also a duty to my own people. And when I look on my people, I see them work and work and toil and labor, and at the end of the week, they have only for their wages wretchedness and misery. When I go out in the morning and see these men standing in their queues and look into their pinched faces, then I believe I would be no Christian, but a very devil, if I felt no pity for them, if I did not, as did our Lord two thousand years ago, turn against those by whom today this poor people are plundered and exposed."

- Adolf Hitler, "My New Order"

During the War President Roosevelt was also involved, as was President Truman, in aiding the Nazis to prolong the war, with the help of Joe Kennedy; to what degree it is unclear. It may be that at some point Illuminatus, Joe Kennedy, being the unofficial Ambassador to both Presidents, was found out to be a Nazi sympathizer and an infiltrator of the Deep State. The Manhattan Project headed by Oppenheimer began several months ahead of The Second World War. There was, in fact, no race to build the first Atomic Bomb between the United States and the Nazis. The U.S. Government already understood the principles of fission by 1935 and by 1937 produced a small scale Atomic Bomb with small amounts of Plutonium and Uranium and blocks of concrete. Nazi German never really had a chance to win WW2 with our Atomic/Nuclear advantage over them. If it became necessary to end WW2, we would quickly do it, and we did. It is very likely that if dropping the Atomic Bomb on Hiroshima, Japan didn't end the war, the use of many more would have been the next step and victory would inevitably be ours. Every scientist at the time knew this, many of them also being Illuminatus', surely would've passed this information onto fellow members who may have capitalized on this knowledge.

One thing is very clear, both the Rockefeller and Rothchild families, its banking institutions, and its investors did finance Hitler and the Third Reich, launching World War III. President Roosevelt was the first to use the phrase 'New World Order' clearly in English during WW2, and specifically when referencing Nazi Germany. Roosevelt used the phrase 'New World Order' correctly, as it was intended:

"Hitler has often protested that his plans for conquest do not extend across the Atlantic Ocean. His submarines and raiders prove otherwise. So, does the entire design of his 'New World Order' For example, I have in my possession a secret map made in Germany by Hitler's Government—by the planners of the 'New World Order.'"

- *Franklin D. Roosevelt, October 27, 1941*

In the previous chapters, we began with the latter half of the 18th century, from the Revolutionary War dealing with the beginnings of a foreign Deep State infiltration of the Illuminati, into the 19th century banking institutions and its further invasion of our finances, then going into the early half of the 20th century with the introduction of Communism being injected into our Governments Intelligence Agencies during Operation Paperclip, which introduced Nazi Germans into the highest levels of our Government (the CIA, FBI The Department of Justice, and eventually finding their way up to the Presidency). The Deep States pattern has clearly been seen as an effort by way of foreign infiltration, to undermine the fabric of our Government. It seemed as though the Illuminati perfected the craft of evil, through the practice of discipline, where Hatha Yoga was used to achieve their agenda. The Order of the Illuminati and the Deep State methodically utilized this practice of self-discipline, that is until Hitler's New World Order took precedence over the Old Illuminati Order. When confronting an unforeseen

HISTORY OF THE DEEP STATE

obstacle or making some mistake, under the Old Order of the Illuminati, The Deep State would retreat, to then come back when an opening to strike again became apparent. The Nazis, however, were more aggressive in their approach to world domination and the toppling of Governments, using minimal discipline in their approach to war, and war-like political tactics. Some would argue they were even operating recklessly in their pursuit of World dominance. The Deep State was officially adopting the means of fusing both the New World Order and Old Order of the Illuminati, while still using a certain amount of discipline, but with a slightly more reckless and aggressive approach in the acquisition of overthrowing the world.

"I think that his (Obama's) task will be to develop an overall strategy for America in this period when really a New World Order can be created."
—Henry Kissinger, 2008

HISTORY OF THE DEEP STATE

"The 'affirmative task' before us is to "create a New World Order."

–VP Joe Biden, April 5, 2013

"The drive of the Rockefellers and their allies is to create a one-world government combining supercapitalism and Communism under the same tent, all under their control. Do I mean a conspiracy? Yes, I do. I am convinced there is such a plot, international in scope, generations old in planning, incredibly evil in intent."

–Rep. Larry P. MacDonald

"Each of us has the hope to build a New World Order."

–President Richard Nixon, February 1972

"No one will enter the New World Order unless he or she will make a pledge to worship Lucifer. No one will enter the New Age unless he will take a Luciferian Initiation."

HISTORY OF THE DEEP STATE

–David Spangler, UN Planetary Initiative

"We are on the verge of a global transformation. All we need is the right major crisis, and the nations will accept the New World Order."

—*David Rockefeller, NWO Banker*

"Today, America would be outraged if U.N. troops entered Los Angeles to restore order. Tomorrow they will be grateful! This is especially true if they were told that there were an outside threat from beyond, whether real or promulgated, that threatened our very existence. It is then that all peoples of the world will plead to deliver them from this evil. The one thing every man fears is the unknown. When presented with this scenario, individual rights will be willingly relinquished for the guarantee of their well-being granted to them by the World Government."

– *Henry Kissinger, 1991*

The New World Order was unofficially formed in Kennebunkport Maine with three very unlikely characters, George Bush Senior, George Wallace and a young Bill Clinton, convening during the summer of 1981. Remember that George Herbert Walker Bush's father was Prescott Bush (his name was changed as he was smuggled over during Operation Paperclip). His son later went on to become Director of the CIA and his political prominence and rise to power also seems to have come out of nowhere, but everything is explained in the fact that his father was a major player for the Deep State. Operation Paperclip wasn't merely about V1 or V2 rockets for the space race, because let's be honest, it was not necessary to smuggle Nazis into our Country, then placing them into prominent positions inside various U.S. Intelligence Agencies; Operation Paperclip was a pure and unabashed infiltration of the State. The Russians did the very same thing, but instead of putting them into their Government, they had them working at gunpoint. It's one thing to have Nazis build Rockets for us, but it's quite another to have

HISTORY OF THE DEEP STATE

them embedded to this day, into the highest-ranking positions in Government, setting them up for life when they should've in fact been imprisoned and hung for their crimes against humanity. Instead, The Deep State gave us a Nazi President. Why? It has already been explained that George Bush Sr. was involved in the assassination of JFK. He is also a very high-ranking Illuminatus. These two ideologies are not that very different at all, aside from the fact that one is race exclusive (The Nazi Order). The Deep State needed to expand upon the foundations of the Illuminati's slow-paced ends to a means. Although the 'Old Order' was very useful in the toppling Nations, in undermining them and overthrowing them from within, yet even with the great speed with which the Illuminati Deep State grew as an Order, the expansion of their ideology and meeting their goals, was just not fast enough.

It is clear that the Deep State Illuminati through foreign infiltration and invasion, had a clear idea for a New World, their world, of course, would only be among those of the elite ruling class, while wiping out the middle class and poverty-stricken of the United States and the world. Money has always been their greatest weapon, and they make this known very clearly, never letting us forget it with their symbolism all over now all over our currency. Anyone who looks at it, whether consciously or unconsciously understands there is a New World Order, it's written in Latin, and even if you still do not understand what it says, you will understand the symbols the Illuminati placed throughout the face and back of the one-dollar bill.

"Time and again in this century, the political map of the world was transformed. And in each instance, a New World order came about through the advent of a new tyrant or the outbreak of a bloody global war, or its end."

-George H. W. Bush, February 28, 1990

"Now, we can see a new world coming into view. A world in which there is the very real prospect of a new world order. In the words of Winston Churchill, a world order in which

HISTORY OF THE DEEP STATE

"the principles of justice and fair play protect the weak against the strong.' A world where the United Nations, freed from cold war stalemate, is poised to fulfill the historic vision of its founders. A world in which freedom and respect for human rights find a home among all nations. The Gulf war put this new world to its first test. And my fellow Americans, we passed that test."

- George H. W. Bush, 1991

The stated objectives are given by Adam Weishaupt's Order of the Illuminati:

- Abolition of government
- Evolution of religion
- Abolition of family and culture
- Abolition of Nationalism
- Establishing a One-World Government
- Population control
- Control of Monetary Distribution

- Abolition of Property Rights

Clear enhanced objectives by the New World Order:

- Subversion of state economies via Socialism
- Subversion of the world economy via Globalism
- Subversion of the American culture via open borders
- Subversion of world cultures via Globalism
- Stated goal of the introduction of World citizenship
- Establishing dominance of all Air Space, including deep space while creating a One-World via the United Nations, when in the wrong hands will be used as it has been stated to be, as the means to begin World War 3
- Visions of 2020 state that after a Globalized economic collapse, it will then give

rise to finish what Nazi Germany started in World War II to be finished in the Third World War.

In the 1950s and 60s, the Deep State Illuminati's vision of the Old Order wasn't noticed by the American public (and perhaps still hasn't been, until now) until we began to see what Eisenhower forewarned about an already planned the Deep State Cuban Missile Crisis of 1962. Since 1963 there have been calls for escalations of war and wars at an alarming rate, much of which can be attributed to the perpetual economic machine of the Military Industrial Complex. There is a deeper explanation for the reason why the Deep State has an accelerated New Order, this time with more specifics, extending the old order. Their agenda now being a globalized one-world economy, coupled with open borders and in many cases, no borders throughout Europe, North and South America and the world; is slowly becoming a reality. This is not just a Democrat agenda, it is a Deep State agenda, and will continue so long as we have a Deep State Shadow Government.

Until now, a precise definition as to what the New World Order has not been uncovered nor stated clearly. Hitler was an Illuminatus who emerged from Bavaria, just as Weishaupt did. 'The New World Order was not the vision of our United Nations founding fathers,' as George Herbert Walker Bush deliberately and falsely claimed it was; The New World Order has always been the vision of Adolf Hitler. He coined the phrase, was a practicing Illuminatus, wrote the book on it, and was the first to put the visions of his New Order into practice by launching World War II. The so-called peacekeeping founders of the United Nations did not create it, and any other account of the origin of 'The New World Order' is a lie. The Rothschilds were heavily invested in wartime MIC and the launch of both World War I and WW2, they even were present for the Treaties as they were a legal document, at the end of both World wars. To say that World War I and II happened all by themselves and without Illuminati fomentation and financing would be a lie. As sad as it is for the author of this book to admit, I too believed these same things, and still, wish it were not true. However, we must confront the truth as hard is it may be at first, moving past it, and armed with this knowledge find ways to avoid being fooled by these fomented, financed, and although they become real; never had to take place. The Military men and women who fought in these wars should always be honored and treated with reverence for serving and saving our country. Their sacrifices and dedication are real, and nothing should be taken from them.

Nevertheless, there will be more calls for retaliation for false flag attacks, but in the future, I believe they will be worse than all previous wars. We will be asked as a Nation by the Deep State (perhaps during President Trumps administration, but without a question after it) to share the so-called common bonds of all major faiths and religions, an increasing need for a Globalized World perhaps with its own global citizenship, always with the promise of peace;

where all nations can come together in peace and harmony, with one currency, one race, no religion, and no culture. The New World Order has set a deadline repeatedly for the year 2020 to begin the rapid acceleration and use of its new globalized New World Order. By the year 2020 According to the objectives of the New World Order, all globalized endeavors, including the absence of all physical borders around the world, and a Globalized Communist economy. The New World Order has stated that once a fully integrated Globalized economy, from the Atlantic (North American Free Trade Agreement) into Europe and Asia and throughout the world has taken been fully implemented, causing instability throughout countries around the world, we will then enter phase 2 under The New World Order. Phase 2 is the fomentation of the next World War and is set for some time between 2020 and perhaps 2025. Ultimately, The Deep State New World Orders ultimate objective is to be an entire one-world society comprised of only 500 million of the World Elite living together in their 'New World.'

HISTORY OF THE DEEP STATE

During operation Paperclip, The Deep State Communist Nazis working at NASA co-wrote a book called 'Visions for 2020', The Deep State is planning the fomentation of a full-scale attack similar to World War 1 and WW2; which they hope will result in a full-scale 3rd World War. As most of you know, as long as President Trump remains President, we are in good hands. Trump has driven back The Deep States plans by at least four years, but what happens after President Trump? Unless he is able to eliminate the Deep State completely; and all of its agencies, which are many, we as a country, as with the rest of the world, will find ourselves in very grave danger.

Eventually, the New World Order achieve their goals with their Deep State Presidents in place, always following their orders. It makes no difference today, just as it hasn't before, whether the President you vote for is a Democrat, Republican, or Independent; since most of our previous Presidents have always been members of the Cincinnati Society, and as I had mentioned before any

President who was a member of the Cincinnati Society is also an agent of the Deep State. Even if President Trump were a member of any of these clubs - what's different about President Trump is that his love of for this Country, his patriotism, and his willingness to do what's best for America is more important than anything else. It's not a popularity contest for him; it is simply about doing what is right for America, respect for the Constitution and founding fathers, respect for the law, and above all he remains fearless fighting a 241-year-old Deep State. A Deep State that smuggled and blackmailed its way into our country by foreign invaders with malice, ill-will & unadulterated hate for our country, our culture, and our traditions. The Deep State are not just Obama holdovers whom you can simply fire. If President Trump wants to truly eliminate the Deep State, he must eventually put away the 3-D chessboard; because he's outnumbered, and will eventually lose, although he is incredibly good at the game; it nevertheless still their game. Ultimately, it is his decision alone to make, but the future of our Country is at stake. The only solution to permanently defeating The Deep State is to stop playing their game and cut off the head of the snake.

COMING THIS WINTER, THE HISTORY OF THE DEEP STATE: VOLUME II OF THE HISTORY OF DEEP STATE TRILOGY!!!

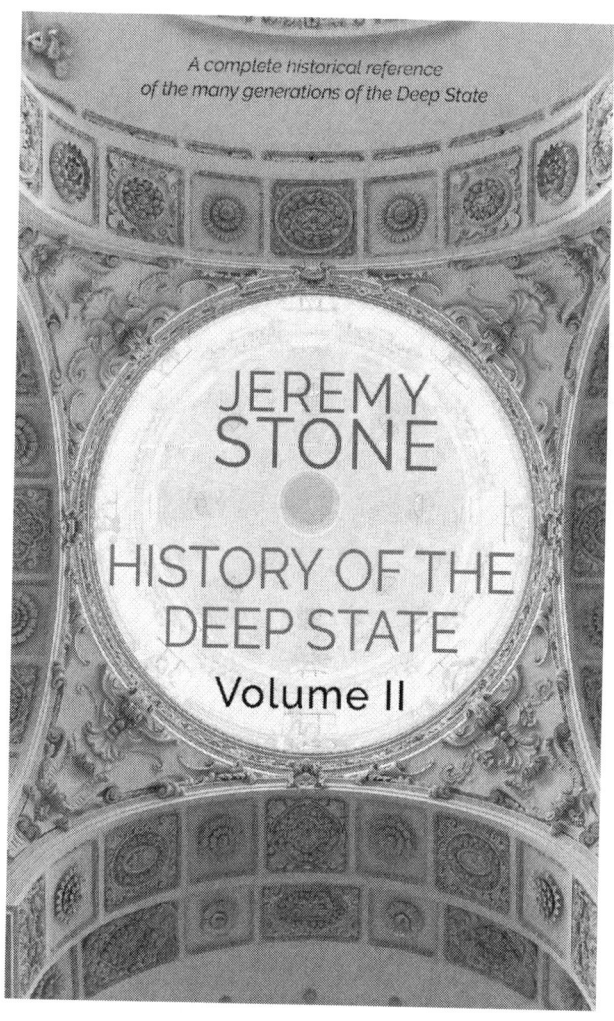

YOU WILL ALSO LOVE 'THE DEEP STATE: THE NOVEL', ALSO THE FIRST OF A DEEP STATE SERIES OF FANTASTIC THRILLERS!!!

DRAIN THE DEEP STATE!

Keep America Great 2020!

MAGA

HISTORY OF THE DEEP STATE

164900
6468

171868
55500

116368

183 ATT
150 DJE

333
118 Front
85 cun En

526

107
30
125

262
300 chair
200 Sears

762

116368
76200

40168